Put to the Test
Tools and Techniques for Classroom Assessment

Therese M. Kuhs
Robert L. Johnson
Susan A. Agruso
Diane M. Monrad

HEINEMANN

Portsmouth, NH

Heinemann
A division of Reed Elsevier Inc.
361 Hanover Street
Portsmouth, NH 03801–3912
www.heinemann.com

Offices and agents throughout the world

The authors and publisher wish to thank those who have generously given permission to reprint bor-rowed material:

Figures 3–1 and 3–2: "Aquarium Task" reprinted with permission from New Standards. The New Stan-dards assessment system includes performance standards with performance descriptions, student work samples and commentaries, on-demand examinations, and a portfolio system. For more information con-tact the National Center on Education and the Economy, 202-783-3668 or <http://www.ncee.org>.

Figure 3–3: "Bowling Task" is reprinted from *A Sampler of Mathematics Assessment Addendum* published by the California Department of Education, 1993. Used by permission.

Credits continue on p. 171.

Library of Congress Cataloging-in-Publication Data
Put to the test : tools and techniques for classroom assessment / Therese M. Kuhs … [et al.].
    p.   cm.
    Includes bibliographical references.
    ISBN 0-325-00278-9 (pbk.)
    1. Educational tests and measurements—Handbooks, manuals, etc.   I. Kuhs, Therese.

LB3051 .P87 2001
371.26—dc 21   00-054046

Editor: Victoria Merecki
Production: Vicki Kasabian
Cover design: Joni Doherty
Manufacturing: Deanna Richardson

Printed in the United States of America on acid-free paper
09 08 07 06 05 VP 5 6 7 8 9

CONTENTS

1 | AN OVERVIEW OF ASSESSMENT

One of the most important things a teacher does is monitor and assess student learning. Flash back thirty years ago and you would see teachers assessing student learning using end of the chapter exercises, worksheets, tests, and the occasional project. At the end of the year students might respond to the multiple-choice items on a standardized test. Some of these practices are still visible today. However, the work on projects is no longer a rare occurrence, and a wider range of assessment strategies are in use. In today's classrooms, students keep journals, make presentations, work in groups, assemble portfolios of their work, and have individual conversations with their teachers to demonstrate what they know and are able to do. This book is designed to provide information about this broad range of assessment tools that can be used effectively in most classroom settings.

The move to make use of more comprehensive assessment strategies in the classroom parallels the use of open-ended assessments in state testing programs. States no longer rely solely on multiple-choice, norm-referenced tests to assess student learning. In 1998, thirty-five states included a writing assessment in their testing programs and twenty included some form of performance assessment (Olson, Bond, and Andrews 1999). School districts have also begun to use more diverse assessment approaches. One of these, the "Work Sampling System" (Meisels et al. 1995), is a continuous assessment approach in which teachers use checklists, portfolios, and narrative summaries as the basis for decisions about student progress. This use of more complex assessments of student performance can be associated with different visions of what students should know and be able to do.

During the industrialization era, education consisted of two systems: one for the elite, which emphasized critical thinking skills, and another for the masses, which emphasized routine reading and mathematics skills (Resnick and Resnick 1992). With the onset of modern technology, employers have come to need workers with the ability to make critical judgments and decisions. Critical thinking skills have become a requirement of a literate workforce. In response to such changes in the workplace, the curriculum frameworks of the '90s formally expressed the expectation that *all* students be able to apply critical thinking skills in the study of content areas (see, for example, AAAS 1993; NCTE and IRA 1996; NCTM 2000). These curriculum frameworks outline the key elements of a quality educational experience for students and recognize that acquisition of a collection of facts is not sufficient in today's world. Current frameworks suggest that students should be able to develop the ability to think analytically, to use their knowledge of school subjects in meaningful ways, and to transfer these skills from school to the workplace.

In response to the curriculum changes, new methods of assessing students were required. For example, the standards developed by AAAS have changed the focus of science assessment by stressing the importance of hands-on science activities accompanied by performance-based assessments. NCTE was instrumental in advocating the use of direct writing assessments in state-level assessment programs and supporting the use of classroom portfolios as an important assessment tool. Similarly, NCTM has advocated the use of multiple forms of assessment that involve open-ended responses, requiring students to explain and justify their problem-solving approaches.

PURPOSES OF CLASSROOM ASSESSMENT

The central purpose of classroom assessment is to provide information about what students know and are able to do. This information is important to teachers, students, and families. For teachers, such information can enable them to plan future lessons that match the needs of students in their classrooms. In one instance the results from an assessment might lead a teacher to spend more time on a topic based on the lack of understanding demonstrated by students on the test. In another case, a teacher might decide to increase the pacing of instruction. In still others, a teacher might decide to divide the class into groups and offer different kinds of lessons or tasks to different student groups.

In addition to guiding classroom instruction, assessments help teachers:

- formulate plans and strategies to support the instructional needs of students
- share information with students about their progress
- collect information to assign student grades
- evaluate the effectiveness of their instructional strategies and curricula
- prepare summative information on student progress for decisions such as promotion, retention, assignment to special programs, and referrals to other needed assistance programs

For students, assessment serves two main purposes. First, the results of an assessment provide students with information about their performance that can promote their learning. After receiving the results of a test, a student might recognize the need for further study or attention to certain content or skills. For example, a student whose essay was praised for its content but had points subtracted for repeated grammatical errors might be motivated to attend to grammatical conventions in subsequent essays. Similarly, a student who perfectly recalled historical dates but could not explain the significance of the historical events could be helped to focus his studying in a different manner. In this way, assessments help students identify their needs for further instruction and study in order to meet their learning goals.

At the same time, assessment serves a second purpose. Many students are motivated to study or apply themselves because they know they are to be evaluated. Any teacher who has been asked, "Will this be on the test?" knows that students sometimes focus their efforts to learn challenging topics and difficult skills only if the content will be tested. With the many competing demands on student time, such as sports, clubs, friendships, and family activities, students may not take time to study if assessment is not done on a regular basis.

Classroom assessments also provide important information to families. Parents can use assessment information to track their child's progress. When they learn that their son or daughter is doing poorly on assessments, they can offer encouragement and assistance or perhaps arrange for special help. Parents also make judgments about the effectiveness of their child's teacher and the school as a result of assessment information that is shared with them. For all these reasons, it is crucial for teachers to create assessments that yield information providing a complete picture of the student's learning.

BLOOM'S TAXONOMY

Curriculum frameworks identify important content and outline cognitive skills that students should acquire in the context of their studies of a school subject. Benjamin Bloom offered one classification system that is useful for thinking about the different cognitive skills that teachers may want to assess. Bloom's Taxonomy (Bloom et al. 1956) has influenced thinking about teaching and learning for almost half a century. Teachers who are beginning to expand their approaches to assessment will find Bloom's Taxonomy a useful tool for thinking about the purposes of different types of assessment they might use with students. The different levels of the taxonomy incorporate the broad range of learning that might be assessed.

Bloom's Taxonomy classifies cognitive skills or behaviors into six levels, as shown in the following list.

Cognitive Skills	**Verbs**
Knowledge	label, list, match, recall, select, state, underline
Comprehension	describe, explain, paraphrase, interpret, summarize
Application	complete, organize, solve, use
Analysis	categorize, differentiate, find patterns, infer, outline

| Synthesis | compose, create, formulate, hypothesize, write |
| Evaluation | apply criteria to critique, conclude, judge, support with details |

Each succeeding level represents a more complex skill than the preceding level. The first level, *knowledge,* describes the basic information that might be studied in a subject. Learning related to this level requires students to remember words, lists, dates, and simple procedures and is commonly the focus of many tests and worksheets. The verbs in the list would describe tasks or activities that could be used to assess such knowledge-level learning.

An assessment task that requires students to paraphrase, interpret, explain, or summarize measures the next level of cognitive skill, *comprehension*. At this and each remaining level, tasks can be described that would provide the opportunity to assess students' ability to engage in application, analysis, synthesis, and evaluation. Teachers can consult Bloom's Taxonomy when selecting and developing assessment tasks. If a teacher is focusing on higher-order thinking skills, asking students to analyze, summarize, or evaluate a specific reading passage would allow the teacher to determine if students could demonstrate these higher-order skills. In contrast, asking students to match state flags with the appropriate state would only permit the teacher to assess the students at a knowledge level, a lower-order cognitive skill. Awareness of the various taxonomy levels will enable teachers to develop assessments that cover the full range of cognitive skills.

CHARACTERISTICS OF QUALITY ASSESSMENT

The quality of a classroom assessment can be judged by asking the following questions:

1. Does the assessment focus on knowledge and skills that were taught in the class and are outlined in district curriculum guides and state and national content standards?
2. Does the assessment provide information about student learning that represents typical performance?
3. Does the assessment provide opportunities for all types of students to demonstrate what they have learned?

These three questions address the issues of *validity*, *reliability*, and *fairness*.

The first question addresses the validity of the test. "Validity asks what a test is measuring, and what meaning can be drawn from the results" (National Research Council 1999, 73). The assessment itself is not valid or invalid; the judgments or instructional decisions that the teacher makes from the test results are the heart of the validity question. For example, when instruction and assessment are aligned, then the teacher's use of test results leads to judgments about student learning that are more accurate, or valid. In contrast, if a teacher has forgotten to teach a particular topic that is on the test, then judgments about students' learning based on test results would be inaccurate. In fact, students are very willing to question the validity of an assessment that covers content that has not been taught.

Using assessment items that are similar in format, difficulty, and content to those taught in the classroom will increase the accuracy of the teacher's judgments about student performance. A teacher who has required that students offer arguments about different points of view based on their interpretations of historical events would miss the richness of student learning if she assessed using only questions that required students to recall basic factual information. To fully assess student learning in this situation, some test items should require students to make interpretations or elaborate on varying points of view.

Reliability is another critical characteristic of any classroom assessment. One way to think about reliability of tests is to consider the example of a postage scale. If you used a postage scale to determine the amount of postage needed for a letter, you would expect to get the same result if you weighed the letter a second time. The postage scale in this case would be a reliable instrument for weighing letters. In like fashion, we say that an assessment is reliable if you would get the same result when using it to assess the student a second time. In other words, a reliable assessment provides information about a student behavior or skill that is typical, or consistent, for the individual student.

As discussed in other portions of this book, students' scores on any one day are affected by a variety of factors such as inattention, illness, or interruptions. In such cases assessments do not produce consistent, stable information, and the teacher should not use the assessment results to make judgments about individual students or the class. Frequent assessments minimize the likelihood that grades for the semester or term will be unreliable, because such bad days for students would have less effect on the grade.

The fairness of an assessment is related to both validity and reliability and is concerned with whether the assessment "systematically underestimates the knowledge or skill of members of a particular group" (National Research Council 1999, 72). An assessment that is fair should provide comparable scores for individuals and groups across a variety of settings. For example, a reading assessment might not be fair for students living in the Midwestern United States if the reading were about oceans and required some firsthand experience with beaches. This assessment would be fair, however, if the skill being assessed (reading comprehension in this example) could be demonstrated solely by considering the content of the reading passage and not be influenced by previous experience with oceans.

Fairness is an important issue when assessing students of varying ethnic backgrounds or socioeconomic levels or students with disabilities. Assessments should be designed to measure the skill(s) of interest and not be affected by the individual differences of students such as cultural background and experience. A mathematics assessment using math manipulatives would not be fair to a physically disabled student lacking the fine motor coordination necessary to work with the manipulatives. A teacher could not make an accurate judgment of the student's mathematics skills using that type of assessment. Similarly, mathematics application tests based on travel in Europe might not be fair to students from low socioeconomic levels who have no awareness of the details associated with travel.

ASSESSMENT: MULTIPLE OCCASIONS AND APPROACHES

More frequent assessment and the use of different approaches will improve the reliability, validity, and fairness of classroom assessment. Judgments or decisions about student behavior and skills cannot be accurately made on the basis of any one assessment. A collection of assessment information from different types of tasks and occasions will give the teacher a more accurate understanding of student learning than a score on a single assessment.

Assessing different aspects of student learning requires the use of different approaches to assessment. Classroom teachers must expand their repertoire of assessment strategies to include assessment of the more sophisticated and complex types of learning that are required by current curriculum frameworks. For example, the ability to design a science experiment cannot be fully assessed by a multiple-choice examination. Questions about an experiment described in such a test would only reveal a student's ability to analyze an existing plan for an experiment; it is unlikely to reveal whether a student can pose research questions, identify relevant variables, and design strategies to assess the relationships among variables.

Recent research also demonstrates that children perform differently based on the form of the assessment (Shavelson, Baxter, and Gao 1993). Teachers have often had children who can provide clear oral explanations of a concept during a classroom discussion, yet produce a muddled explanation when asked to write about the concept. When this occurs there has not been a change in what the child knows; only the assessment format has changed, from an oral approach to a written one. Part of the challenge to the teacher, then, is to use multiple assessment approaches so each child has some opportunities to demonstrate what she knows and is able to do.

Professional groups also recommend that classroom assessment involve a comprehensive system using different assessment approaches. The call is for a classroom assessment program that documents students' progress and accomplishments systematically. This book describes classroom assessment techniques that can be incorporated into such a system. The goal of the recommended approaches is to provide children with diverse opportunities to show what they know and are able to do.

Each chapter in this book describes a different assessment approach and suggests strategies that will support the effective use of that approach in classrooms. Observations of participation in classroom activity and examination of students' daily work, special projects, and tests are all important parts of a classroom system to monitor student learning. Chapter 2 presents information about the use of observation for assessment purposes. Chapter 3 provides a discussion of performance assessment, while Chapter 4 describes rubrics and other scoring approaches that are used to evaluate many performance assessments. Important guidelines for the development of selected-response items for tests are the focus of Chapter 5. The portfolio, an approach that is useful to integrate the information from multiple forms of assessment, is considered in Chapter 6. Chapter 7 provides discussion about the use of interviews as an assessment approach by classroom teachers. The final chapter provides a consideration of how these multiple assessment approaches can be integrated into a quality classroom assessment system.

2 | OBSERVATION

Shana and Lila were talking quietly in the family room as Shana's eleven-month-old daughter, Emily, rested on a quilt in the center of the floor. As they talked, Emily woke up and began crawling toward the coffee table. She tightly grasped the edge of the table and carefully pulled herself to a standing position. Standing close to the table, Emily released her grip on the table's edge and stood, swaying slightly. Emily grasped the edge of the table again and grinned at her mother. As soon as Shana saw what Emily was doing, she got up from the sofa and sat down about two feet away from Emily. Holding out her hands to Emily, Shana said, "Emily, walk to Mommy. Come on, you can do it! Come on Emily. Come to Mommy." As Shana and Lila watched, Emily slid one foot forward, let go of the table, and fell into Shana's arms.

Parents learn that children go through a certain set of developmental milestones in learning how to walk, from sitting up, to rolling, to crawling, to standing with support, and finally, to taking the very important first steps. By knowing the sequence of milestones and observing their child's behavior, parents know how to support their child's efforts in the next step in the process. Encouraging a standing child to come to you, while also being prepared for a lack of success, supports the child's efforts to walk.

Like parents, classroom teachers can use their understanding of the milestones of cognitive, affective, and physical development in combination with student observations to plan instruction that will enhance a student's learning. Classroom observation provides the teacher with important information that can be used to:

- record developmental progress for each student
- evaluate each student's strengths and limitations
- analyze specific problems
- plan appropriate curriculum and instruction based on each student's needs

- compile student records for study teams, conferences, and ongoing feedback to parents
- improve teacher practices (adapted from Nicolson and Shipstead 1994)

Classroom observation can be defined as a process of systematically gathering information on student behavior for the purpose of making classroom decisions. Teachers use what they learn from observing students to make decisions such as when and how to teach a specific standard or objective, what activities to include, how to organize the classroom, and how to assess students' progress. In making such decisions, teachers must make inferences from the behaviors being observed. Inferences are the judgments or conclusions that can be drawn based on observational data. The observation is interpreted and meaning is assigned to it based on the teacher's knowledge and past experiences. The accuracy of these inferences is increased when they are based on more than one set of observations that occur over time. The more information that teachers collect in a systematic way about students, the more confidence they can have that their inferences are accurate.

Every day people make judgments, evaluate behavior, and adjust their own behavior on the basis of their interpretations (i.e., inferences) of what they observe. People observe the behavior of others in their homes, workplaces, communities, schools, churches, and a myriad of other settings. They observe the interactions between others, note the outcomes, and pay attention to the contexts in which the interactions occur.

In the classroom, inferences from student observation help teachers more effectively tailor instruction to individual student needs. Many student skills can be assessed through observation. For example, oral reading, speaking, listening, social interaction, motor skills, use of specialized equipment such as microscopes and computers, and handwriting are skills that lend themselves to assessment through observation.

Teachers have different purposes in mind when they observe students. At certain times teachers may want to conduct open observations and keep track of significant student behaviors or events. Different strategies are useful to record information that will serve the teacher's purpose. Anecdotal records are informal notes used for recording observations of spontaneous behaviors or events in the classroom. In other cases it is useful to have a checklist of particular performances or abilities that a student may demonstrate while being observed. While a checklist allows the teacher to indicate whether a student demonstrates a skill or not, a rating scale can be used to record a judgment about how well a student demonstrates a skill.

The specific purpose of the observation will determine which type of record-keeping system is best to use. The following list summarizes the purpose of each of the three recording methods.

Method	Purpose
anecdotal record	to record important spontaneous behavior in an open-ended format

| checklist | to record the presence or absence of specified behaviors, characteristics, attitudes, and so on |
| rating scale | to record the teacher's judgment of the degree of specified behaviors, characteristics, attitudes, and so on |

Each method for recording observational information has its own advantages and limitations. For example, anecdotal records can capture the unplanned event, but a checklist cannot. Checklists are appropriate for recording the presence or absence of certain behaviors, but would not be a good way to record the quality of the observed behavior. Rating scales can be used to assess the quality of behavior or the degree to which the behavior occurs, but would not be useful for recording spontaneous behavior in the classroom or on the playground. Each of these methods of recording information from student observations will be described in the following sections.

ANECDOTAL RECORDS

Sometimes an unpredicted event is one a teacher wants to remember because it provides important information about an individual student's learning. For example, a teacher might want to remember the first time a particular student volunteered to read for the class after several weeks of refusing to read aloud. An anecdotal record, in this case, would help the teacher document this event for use when thinking about the student's progress or when discussing this progress with the student's family members. Figure 2–1 shows what such an anecdotal note might look like.

It is not possible to preplan categories for the anecdotal record; the only information that would be on every anecdotal record relates to such things as the student's name, the date and time of the observation, the setting, and who did the observation. Note that places to record such information are labeled in Figure 2–1. The rest of the record consists of the teacher's description of

---

Name: *Greg Miller*   Date: *9/17/00*
Observer: *Sandra Polimski*   Time: *10:10 a.m.*
Setting: *Reading period*

Observation:
Greg raised his hand when I asked who wanted to read next. He slowly read one paragraph and smiled. He read each word correctly. He did not use voice intonation for periods and question marks.

FIGURE 2–1   *Sample anecdotal note*

what occurred. When writing anecdotal records, "emphasis should be to events that demonstrate a child's typical behavior or strikingly unusual behavior" (Goodwin and Driscoll 1980, 2). Anecdotal records frequently capture information that might not be documented without the use of this kind of record keeping.

Each anecdotal record should use clear and objective language to provide a factual account that gives information about the student's academic, social, or physical development. Only one observation should be recorded on each anecdotal record. Verbal statements made by the student in connection with the observed behavior should be written exactly whenever possible, *without* interpretation by the observer. For example, the two anecdotal notes below describe the same observation of three-year-old Megan by two different observers:

Anecdotal Note 1

Megan happily sorted through the blocks on the table and picked out a large pile of them. She lined up the pile of blocks using different colors and then made a remark about the work that expressed her satisfaction.

Anecdotal Note 2

Megan smiled as she picked out all of the red, blue, and yellow blocks and piled them in front of her. She pushed the remaining blocks of varying colors to the top of the table. In the cleared area, Megan made a horizontal line of blocks with all of the red blocks placed first, followed by the yellow blocks, and then the blue blocks. Megan smiled as she said, "It's a rainbow snake."

Anecdotal Note 1 does not provide enough specific information about Megan's block play to make inferences about her developing skills in color recognition, grouping, patterning, creativity, or language development. In contrast, Anecdotal Note 2 reveals that Megan sorted three colors from a variety of colored blocks, grouped colors together, and made a display of horizontal blocks that showed a clear pattern. The direct quotation provides a record of Megan's use of language and indications of what she was thinking about.

Providing factual, detailed accounts makes it easier to be objective and to avoid subjective words such as *happily*, which appears in Anecdotal Note 1. Objective recording is important because subjectivity imposes the observer's interpretation of the event on subsequent readers. Thus, when anecdotal records contain an account of the teacher's interpretations instead of an account of the observed behavior, the value of the observation is minimized. Teachers need to practice writing anecdotal records that do not introduce their biases or interpretations. Objective recording of student behavior will provide the teacher with a collection of anecdotal notes that can be used to reflect on all the facets of behavior that were observed before forming any judgments.

Teachers must find opportunities for observation and techniques that make recording convenient. For example, during oral reading or learning center time or as students arrive in the morning, the teacher might find time to write a student's name and something she observed about the child on a notepad. This allows the teacher to make note of the child who reads without error, or the child who is correctly explaining work to his friend, or the child who cries when being dropped off at school.

Anecdotal notes are most reliable when recorded as soon as possible after the observed behavior. Sometimes the classroom may be so busy that the teacher only has time to write a few words to describe the event of interest. For example, Jennifer Weber observed a significant event in her kindergarten classroom as all of the children were arriving in the morning. She jotted down the following key words:

Shemika/crying/Tasha/hug/kitchen

While the students were eating their lunch, Jennifer expanded her cryptic notes into the anecdotal note shown in Figure 2–2.

This particular anecdotal note is important in documenting Tasha's growth of empathy (socioemotional growth), but it also provides observational information about Shemika's adjustment to school and development of peer relationships. Some teachers might choose to use this one anecdotal note for both girls, making a copy of the note and filing it with records for both Tasha and Shemika. Such notations provide a record of information that can be shared with parents to explain the child's strengths and document what the child is finding difficult. Records about behavior often reveal a pattern that helps the teacher understand a child's fears or frustrations so that appropriate steps can be taken to support the child's growth. Of course, when sharing these notes with parents, teachers must omit other students' names to protect confidentiality.

Name: *Tasha Daniels*   Date: *9/23/00*
Observer: *Jennifer Weber*   Time: *8:45 a.m.*
Setting: *Classroom before school*

Observation:
Tasha walked up to Shemika, who was crying and clutching her mother's coat. Tasha put her arms around Shemika and hugged her, not saying anything. Tasha then took Shemika's hand and led her over to the kitchen center.

FIGURE 2–2   *Anecdotal note of observation before school*

The challenge is to keep track of all those little pieces of paper! Some teachers keep Post-it Notes® in a pocket so they can record observations as they occur. They have organized a notebook with a page labeled for each child. At the end of the day, they stick the Post-its® on the appropriate pages. When it's time for lesson planning, a school-family conference, or report cards, the collection of notes taken over time calls things to mind that are often very helpful in making decisions or communicating with parents. Teachers like this filing system because it takes so little time since no rewriting is needed. Using the notebook also makes the file portable. Teachers can easily carry it home, to the teacher's work room, or to the principal's office when they want to reflect on student performance, plan lessons, or do reports.

Teachers use several other techniques to record anecdotal information. Teachers can easily carry microcassette tape recorders and unobtrusively record observations in the classroom or on the playground. Some teachers use a box grid on a sheet kept on a clipboard. The teacher merely writes observations in the box labeled with a child's name when something significant occurs, using a different sheet each week. With a quick glance, the teacher can easily note anyone who has not been observed and focus attention on that child during the next observation period.

Judgments about student behavior should not be made from a single observation, but drawn from several anecdotal records. With a series of observations, the teacher will be able to determine if the observed behaviors are typical or not. The teacher's interpretation of the notes is one source of information for making decisions about changing instruction. A summary of the anecdotal notes can be prepared to support the teacher's recommendations, and the notes can be shared at a parent conference or sent home as part of the student's progress report.

CHECKLISTS

While anecdotal records capture the unplanned event, checklists help teachers focus their observations in advance by planning what to observe. Checklists allow the teacher to record whether a particular set of steps, processes, behaviors, or characteristics were shown or not shown by a student. The information needed to complete a particular checklist can be collected from one observation or from observations conducted at several times.

Checklists can be used for a variety of purposes. They can be particularly helpful when evaluating student activities that involve a product, such as a piece of student writing or art or solutions to mathematics problems. In this chapter, however, we are considering the use of checklists to record information from an observation, not the review of products. Product checklists are discussed in Chapter 4.

Figure 2–3 shows a checklist developed to record observations a teacher might make about language and social development while watching

Student Behavior	Jose	Pat	Rick	Tamika	Vanessa
Date: _____   Observer's Name: _____
Initiates conversation with peers.					
Responds to questions from a peer.					
Asks for help when needed.					
Invites other children to play.					
Shares materials willingly.					
Makes suggestions.					
Accepts the suggestions of others.					
Speaks in complete sentences.					
Follows directions from adults.					
N/O = Not Observed					

FIGURE 2–3   *Checklist for behavioral observations*

a group of kindergarten children during classroom activities. When using such a checklist, the teacher can mark the date at the top and place a check by each behavior shown by the student(s) being observed that day. Alternately, a period of days could be covered by this checklist, with the teacher noting the specific date (instead of a check mark) when the behavior was observed for each student. Teachers can also put tallies under a student's name if the frequency of the behavior is of interest. The teacher should indicate when there is no opportunity to observe a specific behavior, for example, by putting a notation such as "N/O" for "Not Observed" in the appropriate box. This will help the teacher determine whether the specific behavior or skill has not been demonstrated or there was no opportunity for it to be observed.

This type of checklist can be attached to a clipboard so it is handy to carry around the room and easy to find. When using such checklists, some teachers prefer to start each week with a new copy. Thus at the end of a reporting period, you have several sheets to examine, and you can notice how each child has changed over time. Teachers sometimes use checklists that focus on different behaviors during different weeks. By doing this, they can focus on fewer things during the observation and perhaps observe each child more carefully.

Such observation checklists can be developed by looking at teachers guides, district curriculum documents, state academic standards, and other professional materials. For example, based on the review of such documents, a teacher might develop a checklist to use during an oral reading period in the classroom. If student process is the focus of the assessment, the checklist should list specific skills that students should demonstrate in the task. These process skills become the focus when assessing the student's progress. When a checklist is used in this manner, each feature of the student's performance is rated as being accomplished or not.

A process checklist might be useful when a class has been learning about how to conduct research on the Internet. On the checklist, the teacher might list the skills in Figure 2–4. A check (or date) would be placed by the skills that are demonstrated in the student's research activity. Skills that are not checked indicate which areas need further instruction.

The advantage of a process checklist is that the teacher can give it to students before they begin a task. This strategy clearly communicates what students should pay attention to while doing the task. This not only takes the secret out of assessment and makes it fairer but also helps students understand the goals of instruction and prepares them to evaluate their own work. These types of assessments are particularly useful for process skills that cannot be evaluated with paper-and-pencil tests. Speaking, technology skills, science laboratory techniques, and a variety of motor skills are examples of areas that could be readily evaluated through observation with checklists.

One of the characteristics of assessment with checklists is that the focus is on recording what children know and are able to do rather than creating a record of their deficiencies. Such information is critical whether dealing with the most or least accomplished student in the classroom. This type of assessment information supports the accuracy of a teacher's judgment about grades and decisions about placement of students in special programs.

Observational checklists have several other advantages. Teachers have found checklists to be useful when observing students in the hubbub that surrounds classroom activities. For example, the Internet research checklist in Figure 2–4 helps the teacher maintain the focus of the observation. After an interruption, a teacher would be able to glance at the list to remind herself of the behaviors to observe. A checklist helps the teacher consistently focus on the evaluative criteria.

RATING SCALES

While checklists are used to assess the presence or absence of the behavior being observed, a rating scale requires a teacher/observer to estimate or

| Student Name: _____ |
| Observer's Name: _____ |
| Date(s): _____ |

Behavior	Date
When given a specific topic to research, the student:	
Uses an electronic encyclopedia.	
Uses the electronic card catalog for the school or public library.	
Accesses an Internet browser.	
Accesses an Internet search engine.	
Formulates appropriate search terms.	
Maneuvers forward and backward through identified sources.	
Selects appropriate links to other Internet sites.	
Uses bookmarks.	
Refines/modifies search terms as needed.	
Identifies relevant resources from search.	
Retrieves relevant resources.	
Prints relevant resources.	
Comments:	

FIGURE 2–4   *Checklist for Internet research skills*

judge the *degree* to which a student demonstrates a particular behavior, skill, or attitude. A typical rating scale consists of a set of categories, descriptive phrases, or numerical points arranged on a continuum. Each point, phrase, or category represents a different level of performance. Teacher's judgments are more consistent and accurate if the rating scale offers detailed and precise definitions for each level. Several different examples of common rating scale formats are shown in Figure 2–5.

Figure 2–6 shows another example of a type of rating scale that could be used to assess student reading fluency. In this case more detail can be

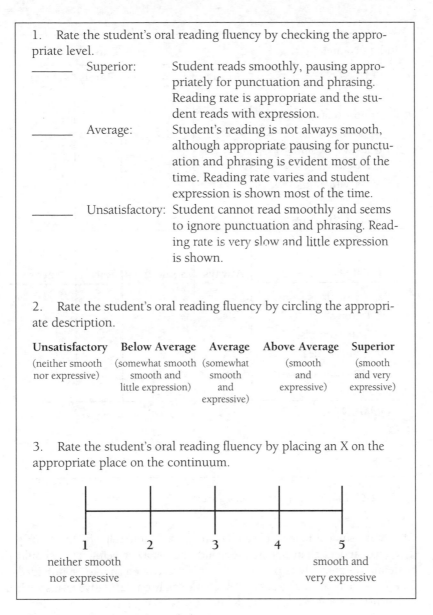

1. Rate the student's oral reading fluency by checking the appropriate level.

_____ Superior: Student reads smoothly, pausing appropriately for punctuation and phrasing. Reading rate is appropriate and the student reads with expression.

_____ Average: Student's reading is not always smooth, although appropriate pausing for punctuation and phrasing is evident most of the time. Reading rate varies and student expression is shown most of the time.

_____ Unsatisfactory: Student cannot read smoothly and seems to ignore punctuation and phrasing. Reading rate is very slow and little expression is shown.

2. Rate the student's oral reading fluency by circling the appropriate description.

Unsatisfactory	**Below Average**	**Average**	**Above Average**	**Superior**
(neither smooth nor expressive)	(somewhat smooth and little expression)	(somewhat smooth and expressive)	(smooth and expressive)	(smooth and very expressive)

3. Rate the student's oral reading fluency by placing an X on the appropriate place on the continuum.

```
|-------|-------|-------|-------|
1       2       3       4       5
neither smooth                  smooth and
nor expressive                  very expressive
```

FIGURE 2–5   *Common rating scale formats*

recorded for each aspect of a child's reading skills, perhaps providing more information to support instructional decision making.

In summary, the development of a rating scale should be guided by several considerations, as suggested by Worthen et al. (1999). First, whenever possible, the focus of the rating scale should be specific, observable behaviors, as seen in Figure 2–6, rather than vaguely defined characteristics.

Student Name:			Date:	
FLUENCY:	Always	Sometimes	Rarely	Never
1. Pauses appropriately for punctuation and phrasing.	4	3	2	1
2. Reads with a smooth flow of words.	4	3	2	1
3. Reads with a quick rate of speed.	4	3	2	1
4. Reads with expression.	4	3	2	1
STRATEGIES USED TO CONSTRUCT MEANING:	Always	Sometimes	Rarely	Never
Makes predictions from				
1. Pictures.	4	3	2	1
2. Letter sounds.	4	3	2	1
3. Context cues.	4	3	2	1
4. Structural cues.	4	3	2	1
Self corrects.	4	3	2	1
COMMENTS:				

FIGURE 2–6   *Language and literacy rating scale*

Observable student behaviors can be rated much more reliably than poorly described student characteristics. Second, the behavior being rated should be defined as precisely as possible. Third, a description should be provided for each level to be rated, rather than relying solely on qualitative terms such as *superior* or *unsatisfactory*. Finally, use as few rating levels as necessary to collect the needed information.

STEPS IN DEVELOPING AN OBSERVATION

In each chapter in this book, we offer steps that teachers can follow to design and implement the assessment approach considered in the chapter. The development of any assessment involves a series of related decisions that affect one another. In reality, you cannot proceed in a step-by-step manner.

We outline the sequence of steps merely to provide a guide for teachers to follow as they plan the use of various assessments.

We consider the development of an assessment to be an iterative process, meaning that consideration of one aspect of the assessment may need to be revisited when decisions are made in a later step of the process. For example, a teacher may begin planning the use of observation with the idea of using a checklist. However, after thinking about the skills to be observed, it may be clear that student performance will occur at different levels of proficiency. In such a case the teacher might revisit the earlier decision to use a checklist and decide to use a rating scale instead.

Step 1. Determine the purpose and focus of the observation.

As noted previously, the purpose of the observation will guide the choice of what to observe and how to record the observation. Sometimes the purpose of an observation is to capture the spontaneous behaviors or events in the classroom. In other cases the observation may be used to assess performance on a planned task or activity. If specific student skills and behaviors are of interest, the teacher would list the skills and behaviors that students are expected to learn. It may be helpful to review curriculum documents and instructional materials to identify such achievement goals. After reviewing these materials, a specific focus for the observation can be selected.

For example, a fifth-grade teacher might decide to focus an observation on state speaking standards to assess the progress of her students in meeting those standards. Looking at state curriculum standards would show her that the following nonverbal and verbal communication skills are expected of fifth graders in her state:

Nonverbal: The student will use effective nonverbal communication skills.

- Maintain eye contact with listeners.
- Use gestures to support, accentuate, or dramatize verbal message.
- Use facial expressions to support or dramatize verbal message.
- Use posture appropriate for communication setting.

Verbal: The student will make planned oral presentations.

- Determine appropriate content for type of presentation and for audience.
- Organize content sequentially or around major points.
- Summarize main points before or after presentation.
- Incorporate visual aids to support the presentation.
- Use . . . correct grammar, volume, rate, and tone. (South Carolina State Department of Education 1998b, 15–16)

After reviewing the state standards, the teacher might decide to plan an observation that will help her assess these skills in her students.

Step 2. Determine how the observation will be recorded.

Once the teacher has decided what to observe, a decision must be made about how to keep track of the student's performance. In planning the observation of verbal and nonverbal communication skills, each type of observation record should be considered. If the teacher felt that individual student progress on many of the state standards could be observed during normal classroom activities, anecdotal records might be the preferred strategy. However, a teacher might feel that a checklist would allow him to monitor students' progress on the standards in a more structured way. A checklist would allow him to determine quickly which of the standards had been demonstrated and which ones needed further instruction and practice.

Step 3. Decide when to observe.

A decision must be made about when the observation will occur. When trying to add observation to an assessment plan, it is important to realize that it is impossible to record everything that goes on. Some things will be missed, but missing a few things is much better than not using observation at all. The teachers who are most successful in using observation seem to be those who designate particular times for observing and recording the information. Some teachers designate occasions for observation while developing their weekly lesson plans, trying to plan two observation events each week, for example. In other words, they do not accept responsibility each day for recording every noteworthy event in every child's day. Rather, they identify class activities each week during which noteworthy events are likely to occur, and they plan ahead to be careful observers and recorders of what occurs during those times.

As the teacher makes plans for observations, she should prepare the materials needed to keep records of student performance. Having the checklist or the materials available to record anecdotes when the class is reading will allow recording of what is noticed about each child's oral reading. Taking an observation clipboard on class outings such as a school assembly will probably result in some notations about behavior.

Some teachers develop their use of observation one subject at a time. For example, they might plan to use checklists to observe language skills for one whole report period and the next period begin observation of mathematics learning during center time. Like the implementation of any new assessment method, planning for observations will take additional time at first. Eventually, however, observation techniques will become familiar and it will be possible to use observation as an assessment strategy in much less time.

Returning to the example of observation to assess communication skills, a teacher may decide to incorporate observation into a social studies unit on the Middle Ages. As part of this unit, the students would be asked to research some aspect of life in the Middle Ages and make a five-minute presentation to the class. Each student would be expected to use at least one visual aid as part of the presentation. These oral presentations would provide an opportunity to observe communication skills.

Step 4. Identify the behaviors to be observed.

For both checklists and rating scales, it is important to identify criteria that are distinct from one another and clearly defined or described. The review of curriculum materials described in Step 1 will provide a good starting point for the development of the criteria. It is important to focus on a manageable number of criteria, rather than trying to include everything that might be assessed. If a teacher attempts to assess too many skills, then he will probably miss some skills while paying attention to others.

In our communication example, a teacher who wants to assess where his students are in relation to the state standards on nonverbal and verbal communication could convert the standards themselves into checklist items. Possible criteria to evaluate the students' presentations could include the following: maintains eye contact with the listeners; uses gestures at least twice; uses facial expressions appropriately; selects appropriate content; organizes content sequentially or around a major theme; summarizes main points before or after presentation; uses a visual aid to enhance presentation; and uses correct grammar. To narrow the focus of the assessment, a teacher might decide not to assess volume, rate, and tone of speech. This decision will help the teacher maintain a focus on selected aspects of the presentation. The characteristics of speech that would not be assessed in this case might be evaluated at a different time.

Step 5. Develop the record form.

All records of observation should include space for the student's name, the observer's name, and the location and date of the observation. For checklists and rating scales, the teacher must spend time developing a recording instrument that lists the criteria to be observed. This advance planning makes the interpretation of the data after the observation very straightforward. If anecdotal records are used, no advance time is needed to develop a particular form, but additional time is needed after the observations to examine the results and make interpretations that relate to the criteria.

The checklist shown in Figure 2–7 could be used to assess student communication skills. The form lists each standard to be assessed and has columns for four student names, the number that would be presenting on a single day. Alternatively, a teacher might prefer to have separate forms for each student or to list all the students' names in a grid on a single form.

Step 6. Try out the observational record.

The first time a teacher uses an observational record she might have some difficulty. For example, she may find that it is difficult to use, does not have sufficient space to enter comments, or involves more criteria than can be

Standard	Damon	Chanta	Shawn	Mica
Observer's Name: _____				
Date: _____				
Maintains eye contact.				
Uses gestures at least twice.				
Uses facial expressions appropriately.				
Selects appropriate content.				
Organizes content sequentially or thematically.				
Summarizes major points.				
Uses at least one visual aid.				
Uses correct grammar.				

FIGURE 2–7   *Checklist for nonverbal and verbal communication*

monitored in the setting. Even though a record form seems simple and straightforward, the teacher might learn she should make some refinements to it. Sometimes the adjustment can be made for use with the current group of students; in other cases the teacher might have to work with the current form but note changes that she should make the next time she uses that type of observational form.

ISSUES

Collecting observational data may seem simple, but several factors can affect the validity of any judgments made as a result of the observation. Teachers need to be aware that their personal beliefs, background, and expectations can influence how they observe and rate students. This is an important issue for teacher observers since the accuracy of their judgments will be affected if they are not as objective as possible.

A teacher's objectivity can be affected by occurrences during the observation that are not directly related to the issue of student performance. For example, if a student who is a fluent reader receives a lower rating because she was disruptive in the classroom, the score does not accurately reflect the student's reading ability. The lower score indicates deficiency in the student's ability to read, when indeed the lower score was assigned because of misbehavior. Conversely, students who are respectful and well-behaved may receive high ratings even though they are struggling with their reading. Teachers can guard against such inaccuracies by being aware that personal factors can influence their judgment and by closely following the criteria in a checklist.

The use of technology and other aides

Clearly, teachers who have classroom assistants—aides or parent volunteers—have much more flexibility in using observation as an assessment tool. If available during center time, the assistant can supervise and assist children, freeing the teacher to observe children and record observations.

Technology can also help teachers gather assessment information. Some teachers have aides oversee and video- or audiotape each child reading. Such tapes make it possible for the teacher to hear children who are having difficulty reading without pressuring the child to read while others are listening. Primary grade teachers might ask parents to provide a videotape that teachers will use to tape a child reading at particular intervals during the year. At the end of the year, the parents would have a record of the child's development as a reader during that year.

Recent advances in the development of micro personal computers (PCs) also offer a variety of options for the recording of observational data in the classroom, on the playground, in the lunchroom, on field trips, or at any other location. Palmtop and handheld PCs permit the observer to make notes or enter observational data at any location and then download this information to a computer for compilation and analysis. Mini and even full-size laptop computers can also be appropriate for recording certain types of classroom observational data. Programs can be developed to facilitate the summarization of observational data so it can be readily shared with other teachers, counselors, administrators, and parents.

POWER OF OBSERVATION

Teachers are constantly observing their students, both inside and outside of the classroom. Most often these observations are casual, unstructured, and conducted without prior planning. Since a great deal of a teacher's knowledge about her students is derived from observation, it is critical that some observations be carefully planned, structured, and conducted to ensure consistent data for classroom planning.

At all grade levels the teacher must make judgments about students' learning and instructional needs in the absence of tangible student work. For example, the sixth grade student presentations on the Middle Ages would not result in a student product that could be physically examined and graded. Nevertheless, the presentations would be important for assessing the nonverbal and verbal skills of the students required by the state curriculum standards. A carefully planned observational checklist would allow a teacher to collect consistent and accurate information on her students' skills to aid in planning future instruction.

Observation is also valuable in assessing the progress and classroom behavior of students with a variety of special needs. For example, observing the behavior of a physically disabled student in a classroom can help determine if the child is experiencing difficulties in the regular classroom setting. Similarly, observations of students with emotional disabilities can provide information to teachers and parents about their social adjustment and academic needs.

The observational records that teachers collect on student behavior and skills are important for several reasons. In just about every case, such records will document growth and learning. For children who do well in school the change will be dramatic, and unique talent and potential can be noted. For those who are less successful, this kind of record is vital. Change will be evident for even the most unsuccessful learner. Evaluation of that change in light of expected learning for that age or grade level is essential to make decisions about the subsequent year's experience for such children.

In addition to documenting individual student's progress, observational records assist the teacher in planning future instruction, selecting appropriate curriculum, improving instructional practice, analyzing classroom interactions, and providing parents with student progress reports. The use of systematic classroom observation enhances the ability of teachers to most effectively meet the instructional needs of their students.

3 | PERFORMANCE TASKS
In-Depth Assessment of Learning

Although some may not be familiar with the term *performance task*, teachers have always used this type of assessment. Essays, projects, debates, and skits are examples of performance tasks that teachers have long used to supplement the information they learn about their students from other assessments, such as multiple-choice tests. Nitko (1996) defines a performance task as "an assessment activity that requires a student to demonstrate her achievement of a learning target by producing an extended written or spoken answer, by engaging in group or individual activities, or by creating a specific product" (240).

A clear example of a performance assessment is the Aquarium Task from the New Standards Project (Figures 3–1 and 3–2). This task requires students to use complex problem-solving abilities by combining a number of conditions as they decide their choices to stock an aquarium. The student must consider factors such as how much space a fish needs, the cost of fish, the types of fish that prey on one another, and the amount of money available. When such an activity is used to assess student learning, it is called a performance task.

One distinction that may be made between performance tasks and the assessments discussed in Chapter 5 is the manner in which a student responds. When multiple-choice questions, true-false statements, or matching exercises are used, students *select* correct responses. Performance tasks require that students *construct* their responses. The responses they construct can be in different formats. Some tasks might require that students do a demonstration, while others might involve an oral response, or still others still might involve the creation of a product. The list on page 26 outlines three different formats of performance assessment and offers specific examples for each format.

THE AQUARIUM

Imagine that your school principal asks you to do a special job and gives you these written directions:

> Your class will be getting a 30 gallon aquarium. The class will have $25.00 to spend on fish. You will plan which fish to buy. Use the *Choosing Fish for Your Aquarium* brochure to help you choose the fish. The brochure tells you things you must know about the size of the fish, how much they cost and their special needs.
>
> Choose as many different kinds of fish as you can. Then write a letter to me explaining which fish you chose. In your letter,
> 1. tell me how many of each kind of fish to buy
> 2. give the reasons you chose those fish
> 3. show that you are not overspending and that the fish will not be too crowded in the aquarium.

Choosing Fish for Your Aquarium

Planning Ahead

Use the information in this brochure to help you choose fish that will be happy and healthy in your aquarium. To choose your fish, you must know about the size of the fish, their cost, and their special needs.

Size of Fish

To be healthy, fish need enough room to swim and move around. A good rule is to have one inch of fish for each gallon of water in your aquarium. This means that in a ten gallon aquarium, the lengths of all your fish added up can be ten inches at the most.

EXAMPLE:
With a ten gallon aquarium,

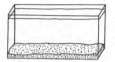

here are a few of your choices:

one ten-inch long fish, or

a seven-inch long fish and a three-inch long fish or

five fish if each is only two inches long.

Cost of the Fish

Some fish cost as little as one dollar, others cost much more. The prices of each kind of fish are listed in the chart.

Special Needs

Use the chart to learn about the special needs of each kind of fish. Some fish need to live together in schools—a group of four or more of the same kind of fish—while other live in pairs or alone. A few kinds of fish have other special needs, which are listed in the chart.

alone   pair   school

FIGURE 3–1   *Aquarium task from the New Standards Project*

Picture	Name	Cost	Length in Inches	Color	Special Needs, Facts
	Zebra Danio	$1	1½ inches	blue with gold lines	Lives in schools; gets along with other kinds of fish.
	Marbled Hatchetfish	$1	2 inches	yellow	Lives in schools; can leap 3–5 yards.
	Guppy	2 for $3	2 inches	red, blue and green	Lives in schools.
	Red-tailed Black Shark	$5	4½ inches	black with red tail	Fights with other sharks, but gets along with other kinds of fish.
	Cardinal Tetra	$5	1½ inches	red and green	Lives in schools.
	Blind Cave Fish	$2	3 inches	silvery rose	Lives in schools; uses its sense of smell and vibration to find food.
	Ramirez' Dwarf Cichlid	$5	2 inches	rainbow	Lives in pairs; rarely lives longer than 2½ years; gets along with other fish.
	Velvet Cichlid	$5	12½ inches	olive with stirpes	Can be trained to take food from the hand and can be petted. Must be kept only with other cichlids.

FIGURE 3–2   *Chart for freshwater fish*

Oral	Demonstration	Product
describing a picture	making patterns with blocks	bar graphs
reporting to classmates during show-and-tell	illustrating math concepts with manipulatives	dioramas brochures
telling a story	finding locations on a map	essays
debating	participating in a group	pictographs
conversing in a foreign language	showing a physical skill (e.g., hopping, tossing a ball, swimming stroke)	journals
participating in a class discussion	playing a musical instrument	creative stories drawings
giving oral reports about books or activities	conducting a science experiment	collections (e.g., leaves, insects, plants)
reciting a poem	performing a search on the Internet	posters written reports

Oral assessments allow a teacher to assess students' knowledge of content as well as their ability to communicate their understandings in spoken form. One common use of oral assessment in language arts is having students do class presentations on the books they have read. In mathematics, teachers may ask a student to discuss applications of mathematics in his or her daily life or tell the class different strategies that might be used to solve a problem. In social studies, students might be asked to participate in a debate or give a speech on an important political issue.

Another form of performance assessment, the demonstration, is effective to assess procedures or techniques that students have acquired. For example, having students show how they use a measuring cup, a thermometer, a calculator, or a computer will reveal their ability to follow procedures that have been taught. A music teacher might ask a student to play a piece of music to demonstrate different techniques in playing an instrument. To assess student understanding of traffic safety, a teacher of young students might have them dramatize the procedures they use when crossing the street. Demonstrations can also be used, in some cases, to evaluate understandings of content. For example, in a reading class, students might be asked to pantomime their interpretations of characters' emotions, thus revealing their understanding of the story.

The third type of performance assessment involves products. Teachers might assess students' ability to collect and record data by examining the tables or graphs that students create. Teachers can assess students' under-standing of the characteristics of living things by looking at the organization of their collections of leaves or insects. They could also assess what was learned on a class trip by reading students' poems or journal entries. The use of products to assess learning may be more convenient than the use of demonstrations or the oral format because the student does not have to be present when the teacher grades a product. The following tasks might be used to assess student learning in different content areas.

1. Write a letter to a classmate who is absent explaining what we learned to do in math class today.
2. Develop a brochure that highlights the main things you learned about the country we have been studying.
3. Keep a journal with drawings to describe what happens each day to the seeds you planted for your experiment.
4. Write the script for a TV commercial selling the services of one of the mythological characters that we studied.

Performance assessment takes many forms and can serve many pur-poses. This flexibility makes performance assessment an important tool in a teacher's repertoire of assessment strategies.

PURPOSE OF PERFORMANCE ASSESSMENT

In all subject areas, performance tasks can lend themselves to the direct as-sessment of the knowledge, insights, and abilities that we want students to learn. The Center for Research on Evaluation, Standards, and Student Test-ing (CRESST) (Herman et al. 1992) suggests that, among other things, per-formance tasks should:

- measure higher-level thinking or problem-solving skills
- use meaningful, challenging, engaging, instructional tasks
- provide a real-world context

These characteristics of quality in performance assessment are illus-trated by the Bowling Task from the California Assessment Program (Figure 3–3). The task involves higher-level thinking skills and asks students to evaluate bowlers' performance and select one of two bowlers for the team. Each student must develop criteria for the selection of a teammate, analyze the given data, and apply the selection criteria to the data.

This task emerges from a real-world context and would be meaningful and engaging to many students. However, some students might know very little about the game of bowling. One of the challenges in developing qual-ity performance tasks is finding contexts for the tasks that would suit all stu-dents in the classroom—an issue to be addressed later in the discussion of how to develop performance assessments.

The tables below show some bowling scores. A higher number indicates a better game.

Dave's scores
152
138
141
144
141
158

Bill's scores
210
105
118
131
105
215

Both Dave and Bill are trying out for the bowling team. As the student coach, you must decide which one should be picked to join the team.

Examine the data and use it to justify your choice.
Explain to Dave and Bill how you came to your decision.
Use charts or drawings if it helps you to explain more clearly.

FIGURE 3–3 *Bowling task from the California Assessment Program*

Another compelling feature of the Bowling Task is that it can be approached in several different ways. The student's responsibility is to come up with a choice and justify that decision. One student may merely look at the table of scores and note that Bill has two higher scores and select him. Another student might find the average, or merely total each player's scores, and select Bill. A third student might examine the scores graphically and note that Dave is a more consistent bowler and choose him. Yet someone who is in a bowling league might begin thinking about how handicaps are calculated and decide to select the player with the highest handicap. The answer (naming Bill or Dave) is incidental to the assessment. The true matter of interest is how the student made the selection and whether or not she could justify her selection.

Although the CRESST criteria suggest that tasks should be framed to reveal the connection of subject matter to events and situations outside the classroom, not all performance tasks do this. Some quite appropriately are connected to assessing the development of school knowledge that is essential to future studies of the subject and may not fit a context that corresponds to student experiences outside of school. For example, every elementary teacher wants students to learn subtraction algorithms, yet, with the advent of a calculator and electronic cash registers, pencil-and-paper calculations are no longer done frequently outside of school.

Performance assessment occurs in classrooms in many ways. Sometimes a performance task is given as a separate assessment activity while at other times it might be part of an assessment that includes traditional test items. Often good performance assessments look just like an activity that might be used for instructional purposes, especially when oral or written tasks and demonstration activities are part of the classroom routine.

Just as careful planning is the key to good teaching, thoughtful planning is essential for effective use of performance assessment. When a classroom task is planned as an assessment activity, the teacher gives careful thought about both what will be revealed about students' knowledge and how student responses will be graded. The discussion below outlines steps to follow in designing performance tasks for assessment purposes. Suggestions and examples are provided to emphasize particular aspects of task development that teachers must consider.

Step 1. Determine the focus of the assessment.

The teacher first must consider what has been taught and decide what the performance task should assess. Recent versions of curriculum frameworks and national standards recognize that students learn both content and cognitive processes as they study school subjects. Thus the assessment should emphasize both the content and process skills that students were expected to learn.

Before trying to decide what assessment task to use with students, a teacher should make a list of the topics, concepts, and cognitive processes that he taught. The specific objectives from curriculum guides, frameworks, or standards direct attention to the content and processes that he should assess. The challenge to the teacher is to come up with assessments that involve a blending of the concepts and skills that were the focus of instruction.

The combination of curriculum documents and awareness of the various levels of cognitive skills will guide assessment planning. We offer an example to demonstrate the steps in writing a performance task. As this task is developed, you will see that the process of developing performance tasks is iterative; a decision made at one level might be revised or amended as you move on to make the next decision.

Imagine a middle school class that has just read *A Wrinkle in Time* by Madeline L'Engle (1998). After checking curriculum guides, the teacher might make the following list about what she could assess:

- connecting the story to personal experiences
- making inferences about a character's motivations
- supporting facts and opinions with relevant details
- examining the effect of literary elements such as plot, setting, and point of view

The teacher might begin by deciding to focus a performance task on the assessment of students' ability to connect the message of the story to a personal experience. Such a decision is the first step in writing a performance task.

Step 2. Decide if you are going to adopt, adapt, or create a task.

Not all performance tasks have to be created. Teachers can often find ready-made assessment tasks that suit their purposes. A natural resource would be textbooks, teachers manuals, and other accompanying materials. The Internet is another useful tool in the search for good tasks.

An Internet search using the key words *performance tasks* identified a host of useful sites. (The authors used Yahoo! as the search engine.) Some Web sites that contain activities that can be used for performance assessment are listed in the Appendix. Because of frequent changes in the World Wide Web, there are apt to be many new sites and some of those listed in the Appendix may have become inactive. Teachers who want to use this type of resource will want to create a bank of sites that they can use each time they need to develop an assessment task.

To get ideas for tasks related to L'Engle's book, we did a Web search for *Madeline L'Engle* and *A Wrinkle in Time*. Quite a few relevant sites were identified by the search. We found one site that had activities or assessments that were linked to particular chapters—<http://www.desconnect.com/ctaylor/Cides/egowman/Wrinkle/intro.htm>—(Taylor 1997).

When the teacher finds particular tasks or activities, she must review these items to be sure they are appropriate. Do these tasks match the content and cognitive skills that are to be assessed? Is there a match between the way a task is presented and the way the content was treated during classroom instruction?

We found several particularly interesting tasks at the Web site on *A Wrinkle in Time*. One asked students to keep a diary as if they were Meg, one of the main characters in the story. Upon reflection, we realized that this task would be a compelling way to assess student's abilities to summarize events in a story and, perhaps, make inferences about a character's motivations. It did not, however, provide a natural opportunity to determine if students could link the story to their personal experiences. So we continued our search.

Sometimes a teacher might find tasks that are not exactly what they need. In such cases a teacher might modify or adapt the task to fit his purposes. In our search we found a suggestion that the teacher ask students to answer the question "Is it easier, in your opinion, to be a conformist or a person who 'does his or her own thing'? Why?" (Taylor 1997, Assignment 3). We liked the focus of the question; however, it requires modification to ensure that students incorporate personal experiences in their responses. We decided to use this task in a modified form to do the assessment. In the next steps we will discuss the modification.

The context of the task is its topical focus or its frame of reference. Selecting the context of the task is a very important process. The following list shows that various contexts might frame a task. The context might be:

- provided by the discipline that is being studied
- based on themes contained in the classroom curriculum
- framed around students' personal experiences
- left open to student selection

Sometimes the context of the task is simply provided by the discipline that is being studied. For example, a teacher might give students who are studying insects a performance task requiring that they make a collection of insects. A class studying slavery might present a debate about Nate Turner's guilt and punishment. In these and other cases the context will be obvious because the content under study suggests contexts that are discipline-specific.

The theme approach for selecting a context is common in classrooms where teachers use an integrated or interdisciplinary curriculum. For example, when teaching a unit on Colonial America, a teacher might write assessment tasks in various subject areas framed in that historical period. Although the study of Colonial America is a social studies focus, a teacher may decide to assess graphing skills in mathematics with a task set in that era. Students could make graphs about imports and exports immediately prior to and after the onset of the American Revolution and make a list of inferences about why the changes in trade occurred. Since the students are already discussing the Colonial Era, that period provides a natural context for a graphing task to assess mathematics learning.

The use of students' personal experiences for task context is also common. If students were studying different genres of writing, their teacher might ask them to interview someone they admire and write a biography of that person. The assessment of the student's understanding of the elements of a biography is now linked to the world of the student.

Care must be taken not to introduce bias into an assessment by framing a task in unfamiliar contexts. As we mentioned earlier, a task about bowling may be unreasonably difficult for students who have never bowled because it is based on some insider knowledge. The context may also be inappropriate because it is not interesting to some students so their motivation to work on the task would be low. Even though many students are interested in sports, not all students are; even though many students watch popular television programs, not all students do. Using a context connected to student experience requires thoughtful consideration and awareness of the interests and experiences of all students.

The context of a task is sometimes left open to student selection if it is not specifically prescribed by the classroom curriculum. For example, a teacher might want students to see connections between number sentences and applied situations. He might give students a number sentence and ask them to write a story posing a problem that could be solved using that number sentence. The student could choose any setting or context for the story. One child might write about grocery store purchases while another writes about a trip to the zoo. In like fashion, when assessing students' writing ability, the teacher might leave the topic entirely open and not narrow it to things being read or discussed in class. For example, a teacher might ask students to write a poem but leave the topic of the poem open to student choice.

As it is written, the assessment based on L'Engle asks students whether it is better to be a conformist or nonconformist without explicitly suggesting a context that should be used as the basis of the argument. Modification of the task could narrow the context. A teacher who wants students to respond in a way that directly reveals insight into the events in the book might ask:

> Based on your reading of *A Wrinkle in Time* and your own experiences, do you think is it easier to be a conformist or a person who does his own thing?

The context for this question is provided by both the book, which is part of the classroom curriculum, and the students' personal experiences. This revision provides the context to assess students' ability to connect a story to their own experiences, the learning goal we selected as a focus in Step 1. Note that the question does not overtly tell the student to discuss the events or story characters in the response, but this expectation is implied. Strategies to direct the student to include information from the book about consequences for conformity and nonconformity will be discussed in Step 5.

Step 4. Think about the task format and what you will ask students to do.

At this point in developing the performance assessment, several decisions must be made at once. The teacher must decide the actual activity students will do and what format will be used. Sometimes the activity prescribes the format and other times it does not. In an assessment of students' understanding of maps and legends, the decision to have students make a map requires that the assessment be in the form of a product. Yet in an assessment of a child's expressive language, the activity of having the student describe a picture could be in an oral format or a written product format. The teacher must determine which of these approaches would provide the most accurate basis for assessing what the student learned.

Often, one assessment may incorporate several formats. For example, students who complete an inquiry into water contamination may be asked to demonstrate their learning by giving an oral report to the class and creating a table or graph that shows variation in the contamination levels at different locations. Having students complete both tasks ensures a more comprehensive and accurate assessment of what students know and are able to do.

Since we know that student performance is often affected by the format of a task, over a period of time, teachers should use a variety of assessments that reflect a balance in format. While a written format may adequately provide the opportunity for some students to show what they have learned, if a teacher only uses written assessments she will have an inadequate assessment of the learning of those students who find writing difficult. In a similar fashion, a teacher who never uses a written form of assessment will not know if students can organize new subject matter and communicate what they have learned.

In the case of our question based on L'Engle's book, several formats could be used. As a demonstration, the teacher could ask students to work in groups and develop a play to communicate the difficulties faced by a conformist and a nonconformist. A debate about the advantages and disadvantages of conformity would be an oral format. A student product might be an essay, a format we will use in this example. The context selected in Step 3 can easily be described as a written task, as follows:

> Based on your reading of *A Wrinkle in Time* and your own experiences, write a persuasive essay in which you argue that it is easier to be either a conformist or a person who does his own thing.

Step 5. Decide whether the task will be structured or unstructured.

Sometimes, an open-ended performance task is very difficult for students and they just don't know how to begin. This may be especially true for students who have never attempted a performance task. In such cases teachers may offer a sequence of steps for the students to follow. Such a task can be characterized as a structured performance task. Figure 3–4 is a structured performance task that a teacher might use to assess whether students can synthesize information associated with a historical period.

By requiring students to complete a set of note cards prior to writing the story, the teacher directs students to follow a sequence of steps that will lead to completion of the task. The task statement also directs students to use resources other than their memories and their textbooks to get ideas and information for their stories.

Even though such a structured task has several benefits as an assessment approach, teachers do not want to use only structured tasks. In the world outside the classroom not all problems are clearly defined. Part of what teachers want to assess is whether students can apply what they know

Activity: Your task is to write a historical fiction piece using the information we have learned in social studies about the westward expansion of the United States.

Using our class text, library resources, and the Internet, make a set of notes about the categories shown on the note cards below. Your notes should summarize important aspects of daily life during this time period. Use these notes to write a story about a present-day time traveler who stumbles into the setting. You must use events and details from the time period in the telling of your story. Make sure to include the important narrative elements that we studied in language arts: a problem, a climax, and a resolution.

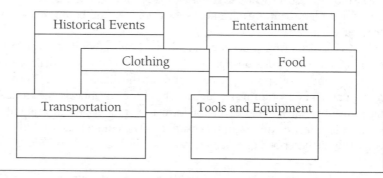

FIGURE 3–4   *A structured performance task*

when challenged by an unstructured task or problem. If the task in Figure 3–4 were to be presented as an unstructured task, it would merely direct students to "Write a historical fiction piece using the information you have learned about life in the United States during the period of western expansion. Include the important narrative elements in your story." Notice that when a teacher gives an unstructured task, it is still necessary to explain to students the evaluative criteria that will be used in grading their work. Just as teachers should vary formats of tasks, they should also vary the use of structured and unstructured tasks.

The essay task written in Step 4 about *A Wrinkle in Time* was unstructured. If a teacher wanted to add structure, he might describe the process the student should follow to complete the task. For example, if students were directed to create a graphic organizer like the one in Figure 3–5, every student would be guided to begin by selecting a book character and a person in his or her life who would be the focus of the essay. The graphic organizer also coaches the student to outline details that support his or her judgment that the person is a conformist or not. By using this structured approach, students are apt to be responsive to the question in their writing.

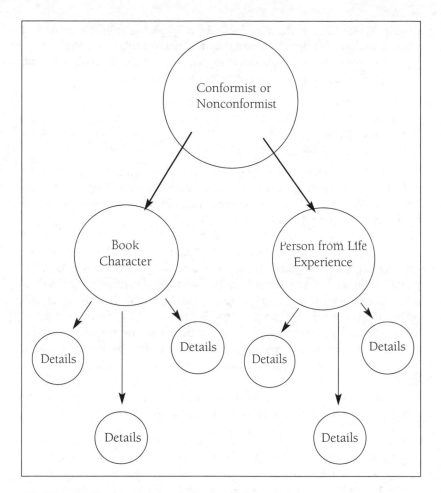

FIGURE 3–5   *Graphic organizer for essay on conformity*

The kind of description that would structure the task will be offered in Step 6. Please note that the example in Figure 3–5 assumes students have had experience with concept mapping.

Step 6. Write the task description.

Once the teacher has selected an activity for the assessment, it is important to prepare a clear way of communicating instructions to the students. In most cases a written set of directions is useful; however, in some cases—for example, when working with young children—the teacher might give directions orally. Even then, it is useful for teachers to write the directions in advance to ensure that all elements of the task are communicated clearly.

Whether the student will see directions in writing or hear them, the teacher should use simple language and sentence structure in the task description. Student performance should reflect what students know and are able to do rather than how well they understood the directions.

To provide students with a clear understanding of what they are to do, teachers should include four elements in the directions:

- task format
- subject matter content
- cognitive strategy
- evaluative criteria

Attention to these four elements supports clarity in the description of a task and communicates the teacher's expectations. Figure 3–6, a mathematics activity dealing with geometric terms, illustrates how these elements can be incorporated into a set of directions.

In the problem statement, the important content that students should know is outlined in the box labeled "Geometric Terms." The task format calls for a product: a concept map. The direction "Draw a concept map" prompts the student to use the cognitive strategy of synthesis. The evaluative criteria tell what will be the focus of grading. In this case the grade will be based on whether appropriate relationships among the concepts (shapes) are illustrated by the location of terms and the connecting arrows. This task is somewhat structured, guiding the student to organize the information into clusters and reminding the student to use arrows to designate relationships.

Returning to our example from L'Engle's book, the directions to the task presented in Step 4 can be written to structure the task for students as follows:

> Based on your reading of *A Wrinkle in Time* and your own experiences, write a persuasive essay in which you argue that it is easier to be either a conformist or a person who does his own thing.
>
> - Identify one character from the book as being either a conformist or nonconformist and provide details from the story that justify this conclusion.
> - Tell how that character's life was easier or more difficult because of his or her conformity or nonconformity.
> - Based on your own experiences, describe a person who is a conformist or nonconformist and how things are easier or more difficult for that person.
> - Be sure to develop your essay considering the elements of good writing: content, organization, voice, and conventions.

The four elements of the task description are present. The format is a product, more specifically, a persuasive essay. The content covers two of the curriculum areas identified in Step 1: connecting the story to personal experiences and supporting facts and opinions with relevant details. The

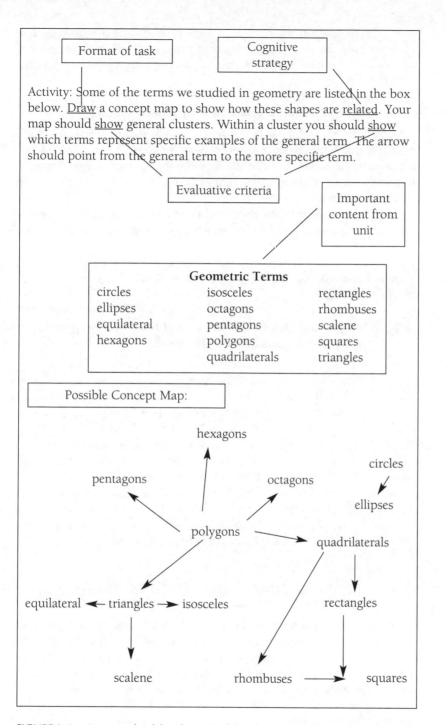

Format of task

Cognitive strategy

Activity: Some of the terms we studied in geometry are listed in the box below. <u>Draw</u> a concept map to show how these shapes are <u>related</u>. Your map should <u>show</u> general clusters. Within a cluster you should <u>show</u> which terms represent specific examples of the general term. The arrow should point from the general term to the more specific term.

Evaluative criteria

Important content from unit

Geometric Terms

circles	isosceles	rectangles
ellipses	octagons	rhombuses
equilateral	pentagons	scalene
hexagons	polygons	squares
	quadrilaterals	triangles

Possible Concept Map:

FIGURE 3–6   *An example of the elements of a performance task*

task engages students in the highest level of Bloom's Taxonomy because they must support their judgments about whether a conformist or nonconformist has an easier life by providing details from the story and from their personal experiences.

Step 7. Plan to grade the students' responses.

After the teacher has designed the task, she should plan how to evaluate student responses. Teachers use a variety of approaches when evaluating performance tasks. Sometimes a checklist guides the evaluation. At other times they use scoring guidelines called rubrics. These strategies will be described in the next chapter.

Whatever strategy the teacher uses, it should incorporate the evaluative dimensions that were specified in the task description. For example, a sample checklist for the essay on conformity based on the evaluative criteria implied in the task description is offered in Figure 3–7. Notice that the criteria in the checklist address the content of the essay as well as the form and quality of the writing.

Step 8. Give the task to students, evaluate their responses, and revise the task.

As was mentioned earlier, the development of performance tasks is an iterative process. After seeing student responses, teachers commonly think of ways the task statement, the scoring tool, or the task itself might be improved. For example, in the mathematics task (see Figure 3–6) some students might have known about isosceles trapezoids and been confused about putting isosceles in only the triangle cluster. The teacher might decide either to eliminate the term *isosceles* from the list or to add *trapezoid* and allow students to use terms in more than one cluster. It is a good idea to revise the task immediately after grading student responses so that one doesn't forget what changes are needed. Often the types of errors students make or the way they respond suggests ways the task or the task description should be modified if the teacher is going to use it in the future.

EVALUATION OF STUDENT RESPONSES

What students and parents dislike most about performance assessments is the perceived subjectivity in the grading of such assessments. One issue in grading performance assessments is that teachers are influenced by factors that have little to do with student understanding of a topic. For instance, the quality of handwriting sometimes affects teacher judgment when grading student papers (see Chase 1968, 1979, and 1986). Also, if a teacher grades several exceptional papers and then encounters a paper that meets the requirements but is not exceptional, the teacher may give the adequate paper a lower grade than he would have given it had he evaluated it before the ex-

NAME:	DATE:
CHECK	**EVALUATIVE CRITERIA**
	CONTENT
	Character is identified as conformist or nonconformist.
	Details supporting classification of character are provided.
	Personal example of a conformist or nonconformist is offered.
	Details supporting classification of personal example are provided.
	Argument is presented about which type of person has an easier life.
	ORGANIZATION
	Ideas are presented in a logical order.
	There is a clear introduction, body, and conclusion.
	VOICE
	The essay contains precise or vivid vocabulary.
	The phrasing of the sentences is effective.
	CONVENTIONS
	Few errors in capitalization, punctuation, and spelling are present.
	Grammar and sentence form are correct.

FIGURE 3–7 *A checklist for essay on conformity*

ceptional papers (see Hales and Tokar 1975; Hughes, Keeling, and Tuck 1980). In the next chapter we discuss the development of scoring guides such as checklists and rubrics. Such tools support consistency in expectations and help teachers grade papers more quickly.

Communicating expectations

Clear communication of expectations takes the mystique out of the assessment process by explicitly defining the criteria and standards that are the basis of grading. Teachers can share this information with students when assigning the tasks. There are several different ways to communicate expectations for performance to students. As we mentioned earlier, a well-written task explicitly describes the details of what is expected of the student. Sometimes teachers give checklists or scoring guides to students with the task description in order to communicate expectations. Teachers might also provide exemplars that show what others have done in response to the task. In some cases a teacher might invite students to discuss the task and develop, as a group, the criteria and standards by which the work will be evaluated.

Some strategies are better in some situations than others. For instance, the use of exemplars can have mixed effects on students. One of the strengths of exemplars is that they build an intuitive understanding of the evaluation criteria. Consider the typical science fair often held in schools. Seeing examples of science projects that model the steps in the scientific method makes students aware of what is expected. On the other hand, if the visual presentation of the sample projects is too polished, students may sense that the appearance of their final products is more important than the content. Some may become discouraged, feeling they could never produce such an artistically accomplished piece. Another flaw in the use of exemplars for performance tasks is that students may mimic what they see rather than using their own ingenuity or creative thought to do the project. If the teacher is going to use exemplars, she should offer a set that illustrates the diversity of acceptable responses. In this manner she might help students recognize and appreciate the potential variability of good work and thus reduce their inclination to mimic the samples.

Classroom discussion of evaluation criteria can be especially effective in some situations. Teachers might invite students to discuss their views about which dimensions of the task are most important to consider. This approach will help students identify the performances that are essential to the task and what will be the basis of evaluation of their work.

These approaches to communicating expectations are frequently used in combination with one another. The task description probably implies the expectations for performance, yet a teacher may also give students a list like the one shown in Figure 3–7 that identifies the areas where they need to focus attention. A classroom discussion would probably begin with the description of the task and then focus on criteria that the teacher has listed.

Keeping records

Since performance tasks assess more complex knowledge and ability, it is desirable to have a detailed record of performance for the teacher's future consideration. There are several different ways a teacher can create a record of performance. One is to use scoring guides like those we describe in the next chapter. When the performance task is done orally or involves a demonstration, it is important for the teacher to plan record-keeping strategies in advance. In most cases it is practical for teachers to assess the demonstration as it occurs, using a predesigned checklist or rubric. In cases where it is possible, teachers find that an audio- or videotape of the oral report or the demonstration is important. When teachers make such a record of student performance, they can reconsider an evaluative judgment with the support of an instant or delayed replay. They could also use the tape to support their assessment of student learning or to look for additional information about what the student knows and is able to do or what the student is finding difficult.

A teacher in primary grades may want to tape-record a child's oral reading periodically during the year. Such an oral record provides a dramatic demonstration of student's learning that a teacher can use during a family conference. It also allows the teacher to reflect on the strengths and weaknesses of a student's oral reading. Sometimes, in place of the tape, or along with it, a teacher keeps a running record of a child's performance by coding the child's errors on a copy of the text the child is reading. Programs like Reading Recovery use a specialized coding scheme when doing such a "miscue analysis" to assess a child's oral reading (Rhodes and Shanklin 1993). Although teachers may not be able to conduct a miscue analysis or tape-record every child in the class, such strategies are especially useful when working with special needs learners.

Many other forms of performance tasks, such as dances, debates, choral recitals, or sports events, are best assessed by videotaping them to allow the teacher to review the performance and reflect on its quality. Such videotapes are also very powerful records of student learning and might be very rich entries in a student portfolio, a strategy we discuss in Chapter 6. Families also treasure such records of a child's development.

Making sense of student mistakes

One of the most important questions teachers need to reflect on is: What does it mean when a student doesn't do well on a performance task? There are several different factors that might have influenced the student's performance. The most obvious explanation is that the student did not learn what was taught. However, it is important to consider other possible reasons for the poor performance, such as the influence of the student's literacy development, her grasp of certain contextual elements of the performance assessment, and her lack of prerequisite knowledge or skills.

Students' literacy development, as we mentioned earlier, may not be sophisticated enough for them to express what they know in a way that meets the conditions of the task. In some cases students who have reading difficulty may not understand what they are supposed to do. In others, they may not be able to organize the information and report it in the expected manner. For example, the geometric problem shown in Figure 3–8 is designed to measure students' skill with space and dimensionality, but the demonstration of knowledge also requires awareness of certain geometric terms and the ability to organize and communicate information in a coherent manner.

The bowling problem that we described earlier (Figure 3–3) involves certain implied understanding because of its context. It is assumed that students know something about the game of bowling, how it is scored as a team sport, and the importance of average performance. More specifically, a student who is willing to take a risk, and who does not understand the em-

**1992-93 KIRIS COMMON OPEN-RESPONSE
ITEM SCORING WORKSHEET**

Grade 4 — Mathematics Question 1

(Learner outcomes covered by this item include: Goal 2, space and dimensionality.)

*The following was included in the general instructions given for both open
response sections of the mathematics test.*

**EXPLAIN YOUR ANSWERS THOROUGHLY. SHOW ALL
YOUR WORK, COMPUTATIONS, CHARTS, GRAPHS, ETC. IN
THE SPACE BELOW. YOU MAY USE A CALCULATOR ON
THIS SECTION OF THE TEST.**

1. Today your teacher put this figure on the chalkboard and asked
    the students to copy it into their math journals.

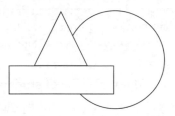

Your friend, Raul, is sick today. After school you decide to call
him and describe the figure so that he can draw it in his math
journal.

In your student response booklet, write how you would describe
the figure to Raul over the phone.

OPEN-RESPONSE 1

FIGURE 3–8   *Grade 4 geometry task from the Kentucky State Assessment*

phasis on team member averages, may choose the player with the highest score for a single game. This selection would typically not be seen as acceptable because those who are familiar with the context of bowling as a team sport would know that consistency over time is more important than occasional high performance. The rubric used in California for scoring this task required that students recognize consistency as the preferred characteristic of performance.

Context is also an issue if teachers develop a performance task involving the characters from a particular television program that they assume everyone watches. If knowing the personalities of the characters is important to completion of the task, a student who never saw the program might have a superficial response or be unable to respond at all. The following is an example of a task involving such contextual knowledge. This task was developed to assess the empathy and caring dimension of personal social development as described in the Work Sampling System (Jablon et al. 1994).

> A teacher might begin by reminding the student about class discussions on taking care of one another. He then says:
>
> "Here are pictures of the characters from Sesame Street. In one group I'd like you to put the characters who you think are nice to others and take care of them. Put the figures who are not very nice or caring in another group."
>
> After the child has grouped the figures the teacher should ask the child about specific behaviors shown by the characters that reflect caring or a lack of caring. Questions should be asked about those who are placed in the correct group as well as those that are not in the correct group.

Example Question Sequence

> "Tell me why you put Big Bird in this group."
> "What does Big Bird do that makes you think he is caring (or not caring)?"

Obviously, children who never saw Big Bird, Oscar, or Ernie might not sort the figures correctly. They would also have great difficulty explaining their sort. If a teacher wanted to ensure that the contextual factor did not impede the student's performance in this case, he might show videos of Sesame Street to the class so that all children would know the typical behaviors and personalities of the characters.

Closely related to contextual understanding is the issue of prerequisite knowledge. Not only do we have to consider the knowledge that was learned outside school, we must also consider whether or not the performance task assumes the student knows something that was taught earlier in school. For example, the bowling problem assumes students can add numbers or find averages; the spatial task required learners to be familiar with terms such as *circle*, *rectangle*, and the like. The issue of prerequisite knowledge is especially relevant when evaluating the performance of a student who has come from a different school, where the curriculum, scope, and sequence of experiences might have been different from that of the current school.

The factors of literacy development, contextual understanding, and prerequisite knowledge can affect *all* students' ability to do a performance task and lead to an inappropriate assessment of student knowledge. When using performance tasks, as with any other type of assessment, it is also important for teachers to monitor whether or not certain groups—perhaps defined by ethnicity, gender, or socioeconomic status—do better or worse on the assessment than most other students. When factors that are not relevant to student learning influence one group of students' performance more than others, an issue of bias may exist.

A teacher often becomes aware that the performance of particular students is inconsistent with expectations based on their previous work or class participation. In some cases the inconsistency may occur because the student did not grasp the content being assessed. However, being alert to the breach in a pattern of performance may help the teacher identify tasks that do not provide an accurate measure of student learning because of the issues just discussed. For this reason, it is important for teachers to reflect on the variety of explanations for a student's performance. One method for exploring discrepancies in student performance is to conduct an interview with the student. The use of assessment interviews will be discussed in Chapter 7.

SPECIAL CONSIDERATIONS

The premise of this book is that a quality classroom assessment system involves the use of a variety of assessment strategies. The one-size-fits-all approach to assessment does not provide a true picture of what a student knows and is able to do. For this reason we encourage the use of a combination of performance assessment and more traditional types of testing. It is also important to vary the types of performance assessments used in a classroom. Certain types of performance tasks may be more useful than others for assessing different subject areas, age groups, and special needs learners.

Using group projects for assessment

Group projects like the following one are excellent instructional tools and provide unique opportunities and challenges to students. Group activities can serve three different functions: the learning of content knowledge, the development of cognitive skills, and the acquisition of social skills. Thus the tasks provide an opportunity to assess student learning in each of these areas. In the sections that follow, we present group tasks and propose strategies that could be used to assess learning of content, cognitive strategies, or social skills.

During the night a heavy snowstorm covered the town, preventing all travel in the city. The electric and phone lines were knocked out by the storm. Plan a skit to show all the things you and your family cannot do in your household as you go through the next twenty-four hours. Also show things your family can create during that time to take care of their needs and have fun. After your group has presented its play, make a list of the tools and machines that your family will not be able to use. Beside each tool, describe the work it accomplishes.

Standard: By the end of fifth grade, students should know that human beings have made tools and machines to . . . do things that they could not otherwise . . . do at all, or as quickly, or as well. (AAAS 1993, 129)

In doing the snowstorm task, students would work in groups and learn about society's dependence on modern inventions. As we mentioned earlier, the context of a task may require prior knowledge or cultural understandings that all students may not have. Having students work in small groups supports success when different children bring different areas of expertise or understanding to the group.

The content learned by individual students may not be revealed in either the process or the products of group work. For example, in an integrated mathematics and language arts activity, a group of students might be asked to use systematic sampling to see if males and females were equally represented in biographies in the school library. Based on their findings, the groups would present their data and write recommendations to the school librarian concerning future purchases. This final report may show that someone in the group could write a coherent report, calculate proportions, represent the proportions graphically, and make data-based inferences about the kind of books that are needed in the collection. However, the teacher would not know if every student in the group had acquired those competencies.

The assumption is that all students in the group have learned these skills, but it is important to also assess individual students in some way, especially if the areas of learning are important parts of a continuum of content knowledge. In the given case, one approach to assess individual learning might be to have each student write an explanation of the procedures his or her group used, justifying his or her recommendations. Another approach might be to use a parallel independent task along with the group task, perhaps examining representation of ethnic groups in the library's collection of biographies. Individual students then would summarize the data and write their personal recommendations without assistance. The combination of a group task with an individual assessment is a useful assessment approach.

Group work can also promote the development of cognitive strategies. Again, teachers should plan groups so that each student has something to offer the group and something to learn from peers. In performing the task, one student may be good at brainstorming ideas, while another student may extend those ideas, while yet a third student will analyze and categorize the ideas generated by the first two peers. In this way group work can effectively serve an instructional purpose; but again, it is difficult to assess the learning of each student during the group activity, and an individual assessment would be needed.

The power of using group tasks for assessment purposes is clearly witnessed when trying to make judgments about students' personal and social development. Because performance tasks are often complex, multidimensional classroom activities, they provide an opportunity for goal-directed, cooperative work among students. Teachers in elementary and middle schools want students to learn to share responsibilities and leadership and to work cooperatively, respecting each person's individual talents. Group performance tasks are a good place to assess the learning of such social skills because they provide a natural context for social interaction. Strategies that teachers use to evaluate personal and social development during group work include observation and student self-evaluation. These strategies are discussed in other chapters of this book.

One of the challenges of group work is ensuring that responsibility for completion of the project is shared. When grading, it is important to appropriately recognize the accomplishments of individual students. Work logs like the one shown in Figure 3–9 provide a tool for teachers to monitor each person's contribution to a group.

In the snowstorm activity students would need to cooperate in planning, gathering materials, and carrying out the production of a skit. The log becomes a record of who was responsible for each aspect of the task. In some cases the work log might document the leadership role played by each student. Such a log would have an additional column to report the student who coordinated the activities of others.

Responsibilities	Student Name(s)
Plan skit	*All team members*
Write dialog for skit	*Belita, Ian, Huynh*
Bring props for skit	*Juan, Margaret, Jane*
Develop and produce sound effects	*Margaret*
Serve as stage crew	*Ian and Jane*
Act out the skit	*Juan, Belita, Ian, Huynh*

FIGURE 3–9   *Work log for snowstorm task*

Any performance task designed for a particular school subject should focus on learning outcomes that are really prized in that field of study. For example, in the study of a play, a middle school drama teacher would probably choose to have students actually enact a scene or a vignette as a performance task. The enactment would allow the drama teacher to evaluate students' ability to read the lines and reflect appropriate interpretations, interact with other actors, move on a stage, and project their voices.

An English language arts class might be studying the same play, but the teacher would be interested in different learning outcomes and use a different assessment. The teacher might ask students to pretend they are the antagonist and each write a letter justifying her actions in the play. This assessment task would show how well students had interpreted the emotions and understood the meaning of the play without requiring them to carry out a dramatization.

In some cases, however, a language arts teacher whose students have difficulty writing might decide to use the drama teacher's enactment activity for the assessment. Through dramatizations, students' insights into the characters' emotions and meaning of the events of the play could be portrayed. Even though language arts teachers would be using the same task as the drama teacher, he would use different criteria to assess language arts learning. The language arts teacher would emphasize the accuracy of the details and the consistency of students' interpretation with the author's intent, not the acting.

There is continuing debate about the effect of literacy competence on accurate assessment of student learning. Students readily object when they are penalized for misspelling, grammar, or usage errors in a class other than English, yet communication is considered a generic academic skill that transcends subject areas (see NCTM 2000). The bottom line is that, again, a teacher must focus on the purpose of the assessment in designing a task and specifying the criteria to be used for evaluating student work.

Making age considerations

The issue of task format is especially critical when considering very young learners. For young children, whose literacy development is limited to oral skills, the task format cannot require reading and writing as the basis for assessment of learning. Oral tasks or observation of demonstrations are considered more appropriate ways to assess the children's learning. For example, mathematics teachers can gain considerable insight into young students' understanding from observing or interviewing children as they represent concepts or operations using manipulative materials such as blocks, geoboards, and Cuisenaire rods.

Assessing special needs learners

Teachers who work with children who are challenged physically, intellectually, or emotionally must design performance tasks that allow students to fully express the knowledge that they have acquired. Many tasks require that students have knowledge, skill, and abilities that are not central to what has been taught but are essential to the completion of the task. When students cannot do a performance task successfully because they have not learned the content that is being assessed, the task serves its designated purpose, assessing student learning. When students cannot do a task because they cannot express their knowledge in the required format, the task does not serve its designated purpose; rather, it assesses abilities that are peripherally related to the content.

As we mentioned earlier, some students find it especially difficult to compose their thoughts in writing. This can be true for students whose first language is not English, as well as for students who have particular learning disabilities. Other student differences might also influence their ability to respond to a performance task. When oral presentations are required, students who have speech difficulties and those who are more self-conscious have limitations that will impede their expression of knowledge. Those with attention deficit disorders, in particular, may not reveal their accomplishments when tackling a lengthy performance task simply because they may not finish the task.

To successfully assess student knowledge for these and other special needs students, teachers may find it necessary to make accommodations in task format. Yet, such accommodations should not change the target of the assessment. For example, if the teacher wants to assess a student's ability to read, then the student must read. It does not make sense for the teacher to give a reading comprehension test by reading the piece to the student and then asking questions. On the other hand, when assessing understanding of concepts in history, it would be appropriate to allow a student to listen to someone read a piece before asking him to respond to questions about it.

To determine the types of accommodations that are appropriate, teachers need to consider the special needs of students and the target and format of the assessment. By way of example, we will discuss a case of accommodating the format of a performance task for physically challenged students.

Students with certain physical handicaps can face several challenges because of a lack of manual dexterity. The difficulty with fine motor skills can impede their performance. Such students face a challenge in recording responses because it takes more physical effort to write an answer and longer to record the response. These students may fail to respond to tasks, or do so by taking shortcuts, because of the frustration they experience in writing. Their answers may lack the detail and elaboration that are present in responses from students of the same ability level who do not face the same physical difficulty.

Teachers might revisit the task format to see if alternative forms are acceptable for students who have difficulty with fine motor control. For example, if written expression is not a target of the assessment, a teacher might consider having the student tape-record the response. If writing is a focus, a student might be allowed to use word processing for responses, thus eliminating the physical impediment but facilitating the assessment of both content and writing.

Another issue related to manual dexterity is that when performance tasks require students to make certain products to communicate their knowledge, the teachers' judgments may be inappropriately affected by appearance. If students experience difficulty in lettering and using art materials, their products may have less visual appeal. As we mentioned earlier, there is evidence that appearance factors such as the quality of handwriting affect teacher judgment. In such cases some support can be given to accommodate individual differences. For example, providing special computer software that allows students to produce graphics and use clip art can enhance the visual appeal of all students' work in spite of physical differences.

The bottom line is that performance assessment can be an important assessment tool for all students. Not every performance task is meant for all learners, but all students should have an opportunity to demonstrate what they have learned in the context of some form of performance assessment. Sometimes the unique needs of learners require that a task be modified; at other times a task can be used very effectively with all students if appropriate support is given to the student who has special needs.

THE CLASSROOM FIT

How does performance assessment fit in the classroom? Teachers have come to realize that not all classroom assessment should be done through performance tasks. When the goal is to assess student understanding of facts and basic skills, other assessment approaches may better serve the purpose. For instance, in an art class, a multiple-choice or matching test would reveal whether students know artists and their style of work. A true-false test in a middle school could be used to assess students' ability to read and interpret information from graphs or diagrams. The advantage of such assessment approaches is that they can be used to assess a broad range of content in a relatively short period of time.

Performance tasks, on the other hand, are appropriate when teachers want to assess depth of understanding of a limited content domain. Typically students need more time to complete a performance task than they would need for a multiple-choice test covering the same material. The following performance task was used in a middle school art class:

We have been studying several artistic styles, such as cubism, impressionism, and pointillism. We are going to turn our classroom into an art gallery. Art galleries usually have a variety of art styles in their exhibits and hanging beside each piece is a placard that tells about the picture. Your contribution to our gallery is to create a picture of some person or event in your life using one of the styles of art that we studied. Also, write a description of what it is people should see in your picture that will help them know which style you used.

Each student will need considerable time to complete the task. Yet, a student's picture and description will allow the teacher to assess the depth of understanding of only the art style that the student chose rather than assessing knowledge of all the art styles. At the same time, the task requires the use of higher-level thinking skills such as synthesizing ideas and identifying and evaluating the overall characteristics of a style of art. Thus the assessment can focus on both content knowledge and how well students handle complex cognitive tasks.

Working around time constraints

Time is an important concern when using performance assessment. Experienced teachers can usually predict the amount of time students would need to complete a multiple-choice test; however, performance tasks are less predictable because of their complexity. Some students may complete a task in fifteen or twenty minutes, while others may take an hour or more to do the same task. In cases where students move to different classes or have different teachers during the day, some teachers feel they cannot use performance assessment because students may not complete the task in the available time. Teachers in self-contained classroom settings usually can plan their day's schedule to accommodate the use of performance assessment.

Two principles can guide the use of performance assessment to help it fit in the classroom schedule. First, for some school subjects and some grade levels, there is a perfect match between the classroom routines and the use of performance assessment. When classroom activities emphasize more complex cognitive skills, the classroom products can be used to evaluate student learning formally or informally. Second, teachers should use performance assessment strategically. Knowledge that can be assessed using other, less time-consuming methods should not be the focus of performance tasks. The more time-consuming approaches should be reserved to assess complex concepts, relationships, and cognitive skills that might not be monitored well through other methods.

POWER OF PERFORMANCE ASSESSMENT

A consideration of Bloom's Taxonomy reveals the strength of performance assessment. Performance tasks lend themselves to assessing learning in the highest three levels of Bloom's taxonomy: analysis, synthesis, and evaluation (see Chapter 1). Other assessments that require students to select rather than construct a response, such as multiple-choice questions, can be used to assess analysis and application. However, with multiple-choice, true-false, or matching items, it is difficult to assess students' ability to synthesize or evaluate, making them less powerful than performance assessment.

Another strength of performance assessment is that it sometimes can provide direct, rather than indirect, evidence of student learning. This difference can be seen in the assessment of student writing ability. Some standardized tests assess writing ability by using multiple-choice items about word usage, grammar, punctuation, and spelling. Such an assessment approach can be called indirect because the type of learning that teachers wanted to monitor was the development of student writing ability, yet the test measured the ability to *recognize* correct and incorrect language usage and mechanics. Indeed, the assessment would not reveal whether or not the student could compose a piece of writing.

A direct approach to the assessment of writing would be having the students use what they know about language usage and mechanics in a piece of writing. Recognition of this fact has led state departments of education to increasingly use student writing samples in their assessment programs (Olson, Bond, and Andrews 1999). Such direct assessment, using writing samples at the state level, has prompted increased interest in performance assessment in classrooms.

The use of performance tasks opens the assessment process to tap more diverse representations of student knowledge. Performance tasks can be designed to allow students who have unique talents to demonstrate their knowledge and ability in different ways. Recall that in the discussion of task formats, we described three possible modes of student expression: oral, demonstration, and product. The student who is not especially good at expressing ideas in writing may be able to document understanding by doing a demonstration or by making an oral presentation. The use of such alternative approaches to assessment can provide more accurate assessments of some students' learning.

4 | GUIDES TO SCORING STUDENT WORK
Checklists and Rubrics

Anytime teachers use open-ended assessments that require more than a simple right or wrong answer, students might question the subjectivity of grading. Teachers can preempt such concerns by developing written statements that will guide the evaluation of student work. Such written descriptions, called scoring guides, are useful tools because they outline what teachers expect to see in student responses. These expectations list important knowledge and skills to be used as evaluative criteria in grading students' work.

A checklist is the simplest form of scoring guide. In Chapter 2, we focused on the use of checklists for recording information from an observation. In this chapter, our discussion will address checklists designed to evaluate student products. In both cases the checklist outlines evaluative criteria for assessing student learning. Beside each criterion is a space to indicate whether that criterion has been met or not. Figure 4–1 is a checklist for evaluating limericks written by third-grade students. It contains the important elements that students studied as characteristic of a well-written limerick. Notice the place in front of each criterion that can be checked if the student's limerick shows evidence of proficiency.

Clearly there is little question about the first criterion: A student's limerick either has five lines or it doesn't. Some of the other criteria, however, might be met to different degrees. For example, what if a student had one

---

Student Name:	**Date:**
___ Has five lines.	___ Has correct capitalization.
___ Tells a funny story.	___ Has correct punctuation.
___ Has correct rhyming pattern.	___ Contains descriptive words.

FIGURE 4–1 *Limerick checklist*

capitalization error, had forgotten one comma, or had used only one descriptive word? Should she get credit or not?

Perhaps the teacher would want to award a different number of points to reflect the different levels of proficiency students might demonstrate. To do this, the checklist could be revised to be a different kind of scoring tool, a point-allocated checklist, as shown in Figure 4–2. A point-allocated checklist indicates the number of points for each criterion. In this example, one point would be awarded for the first criterion, but up to three points could be earned for each of the other criteria.

Using this point-allocated checklist allows the teacher to award partial credit depending on the student's level of proficiency. The levels of proficiency are implicit, rather than explicit because the list does not provide descriptions for how one, two, or three points are to be awarded. The teacher must decide, for example, how many and what kind of descriptive words merit a score of 3 rather than 2. Yet the student is unaware of the teacher's implicit rule. Thus, when using this type of point-allocated checklist, teachers frequently find themselves justifying their decisions to students about how many points they awarded.

The remedy to this situation is a scoring tool that combines evaluative criteria with scales that explicitly define standards of performance. This type of tool is called a rubric. Figure 4–3 illustrates the detail needed to turn the point-allocated checklist in Figure 4–2 into a rubric. In this case the scoring guide is called an analytic rubric because there are separate scales for each evaluative criterion.

This example illustrates many of the things teachers must consider in developing a rubric. Not only must the teacher select the evaluative criteria,

Student Name:	**Date:**
1 point	**Score**
Has five lines.	_____ point
3 points each	
Tells a funny story.	_____ point(s)
Has correct rhyming pattern.	_____ point(s)
Has correct capitalization.	_____ point(s)
Has correct punctuation.	_____ point(s)
Contains descriptive words.	_____ point(s)
	_____ **Total**

FIGURE 4–2   *Point-allocated checklist for limericks*

Student Name:	Date:		
Criteria	Scales		
Has five lines.	**0** Limerick does not have 5 lines.	**1** Limerick has 5 lines.	
Tells a funny story.	**1** The story that the limerick tells is incomplete *and* is not funny.	**2** The story that the limerick tells is incomplete *or* is not funny.	**3** The story that the limerick tells is complete *and* funny.
Has correct rhyming pattern.	**1** Limerick does not rhyme.	**2** Limerick has some rhymes, but the rhyming pattern is not correct.	**3** Limerick has correct rhyming pattern (AABBA).
Has correct capitalization.	**1** Capitals are not used or are used incorrectly.	**2** Capitals are sometimes correctly used.	**3** Capitals are correctly used in the poem and title.
Has correct punctuation.	**1** Limerick is not punctuated or is punctuated incorrectly.	**2** Limerick has some correct punctuation.	**3** Limerick is correctly punctuated.
Contains descriptive words.	**1** Specific nouns, adjectives, and adverbs to paint a picture for the reader are not used.	**2** The selection of specific nouns, adjectives, and adverbs to paint a picture for the reader is attempted.	**3** Specific nouns, adjectives, and adverbs to paint a picture for the reader are effectively selected.

FIGURE 4–3 *Analytic rubric for scoring limericks*

she must also develop a scale. In developing the scale, the teacher must decide how many levels of performance to define and write descriptions that clearly and appropriately outline expectations for the different levels of performance. By combining numbers and descriptions, the teacher explicitly defines standards of performance that she will use in grading student work.

As was the case in the point-allocated checklist (Figure 4–2), two different scales are used in this analytic rubric. A scale with two levels (0 or 1) is used to indicate whether the student's work followed the convention of a limerick having five lines. For the other evaluative criteria, three-point scales describe levels of student proficiency. Also note that the descriptions of each criterion address the same elements at each proficiency level to define what would be excellent, satisfactory, or unsatisfactory performance. For example, the description for "Tells a funny story" talks about completeness and humor at each level of performance. We will use the term *parallel structure* to refer to the practice of repeating the elements of performance across all proficiency levels of a criterion.

In an analytic approach, several scores are given for each piece of work. If the scores are to provide teachers, students, or parents with feedback about specific skills that need improvement, then a checklist or analytic rubric is very useful. For example, the scores from the analytic rubric for the limerick could tell one student that she has strength in the use of descriptive words but still needs to work on punctuation while telling another student that he needs to use the correct rhyming pattern but his limerick is punctuated correctly. A teacher can use this detailed information in planning future lessons for the class or particular experiences for individuals.

If the purpose of the evaluation is to provide a description of the student's performance at the end of a unit of study, a holistic approach to scoring is sometimes useful. Figure 4–4 illustrates a holistic rubric that could also be used to evaluate students' limericks. All the criteria addressed in the checklist (Figure 4–1) and the analytic rubric (Figure 4–3) are also addressed in this holistic rubric. The difference is that, when using the holistic rubric, the teacher must make a single judgment—that is, award a single score—about student learning while considering all of the different criteria that she is evaluating. For this reason some teachers find the use of holistic scoring more difficult than an analytic approach.

The holistic rubric also illustrates the use of proficiency labels for each level of the scale: Expert, Accomplished, and Novice. Some teachers use only the labels, others use a combination of numbers and labels, and still others use only a number or score for each level. When numbers are used, higher numbers should indicate better levels of performance to facilitate grading and record keeping.

Holistic rubrics are very useful when it is difficult to separate evaluative criteria in scoring a student response. For some tasks it is better to consider criteria in combination because they are dependent on one another. For example, students might be asked to write a fictional story. In grading student work, the teacher would want to consider if students' writings included the major components of a story: character, setting, conflict, climax, and resolution. The potential evaluative criteria of conflict, climax, and resolution are intertwined. If an analytic rubric were used, the teacher would have difficulty scoring for the presence of a resolution when a student paper doesn't

Proficiency Levels	Descriptions
Expert	The limerick tells a complete and funny story. Specific nouns, adjectives, and adverbs paint a picture for the reader. The limerick has the correct number of lines and rhyming pattern. Punctuation and capitalization are correct.
Accomplished	The limerick is characterized by *most* of the following statements. It may tell a story that is either complete or funny. The use of some specific nouns, adjectives, and adverbs create a picture for the reader. The limerick has either the correct number of lines or the correct rhyming pattern. There are few punctuation and capitalization errors.
Novice	The limerick needs to be written in a way that tells a complete and funny story. To paint a picture for the reader, the limerick needs to contain specific nouns, adjectives, and adverbs. The limerick needs to have five lines and a rhyming pattern of AABBA. Punctuation and capitalization need correction.

FIGURE 4–4   *Holistic rubric for scoring limericks*

really present a conflict. A holistic rubric, like the one in Figure 4–5, would simplify the evaluation.

Up to this point the example checklists and rubrics have been rather specific. The scoring tools are useful either to evaluate student ability to write a limerick or to write fiction. Rubrics can be written for a specific task, as in the previous examples, or can be designed to evaluate a broader range of student work. The latter type of rubric is often referred to as generic. For example, in writing, many experts advocate the evaluation of all writing genres using the criteria of style, conventions, and organization. A teacher could develop a generic rubric to evaluate different forms of writing considering these criteria.

In mathematics there are also certain skills evidenced in good work whether the content of the task is related to geometry, number concepts, or some other area of mathematics. The ability to communicate in mathematics is one area where a generic rubric might be used. Figure 4–6 is a generic rubric that a teacher could use to evaluate a student's ability to communicate in mathematics regardless of the specific task being performed. Readers may want to use this rubric to evaluate student work on the geometry task in Chapter 3 (Figure 3–8). This communication rubric is holistic but the ana-

Proficiency Levels	Description
Level 5	The main elements of a fictional story are present. Descriptive language establishes the setting. The main character is well developed and faces a conflict. The story comes to a climax, and the resolution of the conflict flows from the story.
Level 4	The main elements are present; however, either character or setting is not well developed. The main character faces a conflict. The story comes to a climax, and the resolution of the conflict flows from the story.
Level 3	The main elements are present but not well developed. Characters, setting, conflict, climax, and resolution need elaboration.
Level 2	Some of the major elements of the story are missing.
Level 1	Most of the major elements are missing.

FIGURE 4–5   *Holistic rubric for evaluating fiction writing*

Accomplished (3)

- Consistently uses mathematics terms and symbols with few inaccuracies.
- Presents comprehensive and clear explanations using examples or illustrations when appropriate.
- Offers discussion in an organized and logical sequence.

Developing (2)

- Uses math terms and symbols most of the time but some are inaccurate or incorrect.
- Offers correct explanations but statements are unclear or incomplete and examples are either missing or are incorrect.
- Responses may be somewhat disorganized.

Not Yet (1)

- Uses terms and symbols incorrectly or relies on everyday words instead of math terminology.
- Explanations and examples are incorrect or not relevant.
- Order of discussion may be confusing.

FIGURE 4–6   *Generic rubric for communication in mathematics*

lytic approach can also be used for generic rubrics. Notice the parallel structure of the rubric in Figure 4–6. Each element of performance that is to be considered is mentioned in the description of every level of the rubric.

In contrast, a task-specific rubric can be used only to evaluate responses to a single specific task or project that students are doing. Such rubrics are often useful to evaluate major projects that are done over a period of time or tasks that assess many dimensions of student learning. Figure 4–7 offers a mathematics task with a task-specific rubric that would be used to evaluate student responses to the task. This is an analytic rubric, but the holistic ap-

Activity: We have a record of daily rainfall throughout the year. Use this information to calculate the average rainfall for each month. Create a bar graph to show the average amount of rainfall for May, June, July, August, and September. Begin the graph with May and end with September. Answer the following questions based on your graph:

Which month had the most rain? Which month had the least rain?

Our city's water department wants to predict when people will be watering their lawns and gardens. Using the information from your graph, tell which month you think people will probably need to water their lawns and explain your prediction.

Organization of Thoughts	Accuracy of Calculations	Presentation of Bar Graph
3: Answers the questions appropriately and supports predictions based on the graph.	3: Calculations are based on the daily information for each month and are accurate.	3: Bar graph is organized with a title and legends, the data are sequenced by months, and the length of bars is correct.
2: The answers and predictions are consistent with the information in the bar graph, but predictions are not clear or correct.	2: Calculations are based on the daily information for each month and most calculations are accurate.	2: Bar graph has a few mistakes in title, legends, sequence of months, or length of bars.
1: Some answers and predictions are incorrect or are not related to the information in the bar graph.	1: Calculations are based on the daily information for each month. Need to continue to work on accuracy.	1: Bar graph has several mistakes in title, legend, sequence of months, or length of bars.
0: Does not write any statements based on the bar graph.	0: No attempt made.	0: No attempt made.

FIGURE 4–7 *Performance task and task-specific rubric*

proach could also be used. Although the evaluative criteria—organization of thoughts, accuracy of calculations, presentation of a bar graph—could apply to many tasks done in a mathematics classroom, the elements used in the descriptors refer specifically to requirements of the rainfall task, for example, checking to see if calculations are accurate for each month.

PURPOSE OF RUBRICS AND CHECKLISTS

Rubrics and checklists are powerful tools that help teachers improve assessment of learning. One way that these scoring guides improve assessment is by ensuring that each student's paper will be judged using the same criteria. The explicit statement of expectations for student learning provided in the checklists and rubrics dealing with limericks reminds the teacher to look at capitalization, punctuation, and the rhyming pattern on each student's limerick.

A rubric that explicitly outlines the content that teachers are to focus on supports a teacher's consistency in scoring. Teachers have all experienced the frustration of wondering whether they graded the twenty-fifth student paper in the same way they graded the first paper. The scale in a rubric guides the teacher to award the same number of points to papers that have the same strength or flaw, whether it's the first or the last paper graded.

A rubric also helps a teacher sustain consistent attention to the evaluative criteria. Without a rubric, a teacher may be tempted to give a very low grade to a piece of writing that is riddled with spelling or mechanics problems even though the content and organization of the paper surpasses that of other essays being graded. Use of a rubric reminds the teacher of the relative importance of each criterion and limits the number of points that a student may lose for any one type of error.

Rubrics can also have instructional implications. Ideally, the teacher should develop a rubric before instruction begins. Imagine a teacher sitting down to plan a week's lessons for language arts, realizing that the work students will submit on Friday will be evaluated using the analytic rubric for limericks (Figure 4–3). In preparation for that week's classes, the teacher would plan activities to emphasize ideas about a limerick's length, story line, rhyming pattern, capitalization, punctuation, and descriptive words. In this situation the rubric can function as a quick summary of important knowledge and skills to be taught during the week and can help the teacher plan lessons that target important content.

The reality of most classrooms, however, is that teachers usually develop the assessments when the unit is nearly finished. When teaching the same content in subsequent years, the teacher will have last year's rubric to support planning. By reviewing or designing the rubric prior to giving students an assessment task, the teacher can determine if she has addressed the important content and process skills. She might offer additional lessons to cover any gaps in instruction after checking the rubric.

Rubrics also have the potential to enhance learning in several ways. When a teacher gives both the rubric and task at the same time, the rubric serves to direct student attention to the important concepts and skills that they should demonstrate in completing the task. However, teachers should not assume that students naturally understand how to use or interpret rubrics. It is likely that they will need guidance in learning how to use the rubric as an aid in structuring their initial responses and revising their work. Two approaches can help students use rubrics to improve their work.

First, having students construct a checklist can help them develop an understanding of evaluative criteria and how those criteria apply to their work. When initially assigning the project, the teacher might ask students: "When we are finished with this project, what will the really good ones look like? What things have we been learning that you might use in this project? What can you look for when you are done with your work to see if you have done well? Let's create a list of what you would see in a good project."

In this discussion the teacher is helping students develop a very sophisticated concept, the idea of evaluative criteria. Initially, students are likely to have difficulty coming up with descriptors (criteria). When students work to develop checklists, they begin to see what the teacher notices when grading papers. The students come to understand that pieces of work have certain characteristics that are connected to quality. They begin to develop an understanding of evaluative criteria.

When asked to develop such checklists for the first time, children may be preoccupied with effort as a criterion. They might say a product would be good, "if I tried really hard." Other characteristics that students identify at first relate to surface features, such as neatness, and obvious ones, such as the right answer on a math paper. Teacher probing or suggestions will lead to an expansion of students' understanding of important criteria and, over time, will lead students to develop insight into more sophisticated characteristics of good work.

Another beneficial classroom activity is having students use checklists to evaluate their own work or the work of peers. Once students have developed an understanding of evaluative criteria, they can begin to look at their work to identify instances where a specific skill is demonstrated. This is an important ability because it is key for students to be able to examine and reflect on their own work.

As students first begin to learn to apply checklists to their own work, it may be useful for teachers to use interviews or conferences to determine whether a child is able to use this new skill. For those students who are having difficulty in using checklists, teachers may use the conference to guide the student in applying the checklist to his work.

A special benefit comes about when students review the work of peers. As students examine the work of others, they come to understand, appreciate, and perhaps learn about strategies and approaches other students use in their work. The use of peer review, however, is psychologically and socially difficult for some learners. To promote this activity as a positive experience, the teacher might propose the task as a treasure hunt in which the job is to look at a peer's work and find instances where the criteria have been met. Deficiencies might be noted as suggestions for revision.

In the same spirit, some teachers use "three pluses and a wish" in authors circles (Mills 1990), guiding students to find three strengths in a piece of work and recognize one way it can be improved. The use of this strategy ensures that students get positive feedback from peers as well as suggestions for improvement.

STEPS IN CONSTRUCTING RUBRICS AND CHECKLISTS

To assist you in creating scoring guides for use in your classroom, we offer the following steps. In this discussion a rubric will be used for grading the oral and written responses to the measurement task below.

> Make a scale drawing of one of the rooms in your house. You are to select a scale that is appropriate for the size of the graph paper. Show important features of the room, such as doors and windows, using the symbols we learned about in class. Show the placement of furniture or appliances, also drawn to scale, and label them. Prepare to describe and explain your drawing to a small group of students next week. During your presentation, be sure to talk about the measurements of at least five features of the room.

Step 1. Decide what evaluative criteria are central to the task(s) to be graded.

The following is a list of tips that are useful for selecting evaluative criteria.

1. Make sure your expectations match curriculum standards.
2. Imagine what a good student response would look like.
3. Think about parts of the task students would find difficult.
4. Make sure that criteria are consistent with task directions.
5. Decide which task features will not be assessed.
6. Limit the number of criteria.
7. Decide whether the rubric will be specific or generic.

The first thing to consider are the curriculum standards or guides for the subject area. For the measurement task, the *Principles and Standards for School Mathematics* (NCTM 2000) would be useful to consult. The teacher should also consider what a good student paper and presentation would be like. The teacher might ask, "What do I expect to see in a good performance or product?" Based on prior experiences and current expectations, the teacher creates a mental image of what students will be able to do. At the same time the teacher should think about parts of the task that students might find difficult. Such reflection would identify weaknesses in student responses and areas where further instruction would be beneficial.

The teacher should also consider the directions she has given to students as she develops evaluative criteria. For example, in the measurement task it would be unfair to use criteria related to the form or format of an answer—for example, meters and centimeters instead of feet and inches—unless such expectations were communicated to students in the task description. Sometimes, however, expectations are established as a classroom convention for all assignments, such as labeling all answers in mathematics, and need not be repeated in the directions. In short, a close match between the task description and the rubric is important.

The fifth tip suggests that teachers deliberately decide what will *not* be considered in the evaluation. Students can be overwhelmed with having too many criteria to consider as they complete tasks. Limiting the number of criteria allows them to focus on the really important learning outcomes. Teachers also benefit because their focus is on the most important areas of learning, so grading becomes less cumbersome.

Evaluative criteria that a teacher might use to grade student responses to the measurement task are shown in the following lists.

The Drawing
- accurate measurement with appropriate units
- appropriate use of a reasonable scale
- appropriate form showing title, scale key, labels, architectural notations
- neatness

The Presentation
- use of appropriate measurement terms
- accurate description of the measurements of five features in the drawing

Notice, criteria are defined for both the written product and the oral presentation. In developing this list, we reviewed NCTM Standards, thought about what good student responses would be like, and anticipated mistakes students might make. After writing the task and then thinking about student responses, it became clear that to assess students' work, the teacher would need to know what each item in the scale drawing represents. Thus, we added the requirement that pieces of furniture be labeled.

Also, the original task only had a written component. Students' verbal interpretation of the scale drawing also seemed to be an important dimension of the assessment. The scale drawing alone would not tell whether students could use appropriate measurement terms, thus we added an oral presentation to the task. We selected an oral presentation rather than a written explanation to reduce the reliance on students' writing skills in this assessment of mathematics knowledge and ability.

In developing any rubric, it is important to consider whether or not to assess surface features such as handwriting, spelling, grammar, and neatness. In the case of scale drawings, we included neatness in the list of evaluative criteria. A decision may be made later to eliminate this criterion or to make it count for fewer points than other criteria.

Another matter to consider is whether the rubric is being designed to grade a single specific task (a task-specific rubric) or if it will be used repeatedly to grade different pieces of student work (a generic rubric). The decision about whether the rubric will be generic or task-specific influences the definition of evaluative criteria, a matter considered in Step 3. A task-specific rubric will be developed here; thus the focus will be only on measurement skills associated with a scale drawing of a room.

Step 2. Decide if the student work will be evaluated holistically or analytically.

As we mentioned earlier, the choice of analytic or holistic approaches is influenced by the intended purpose of the assessment. If the purpose is to provide an overall assessment that integrates the different elements of student performance, a holistic rubric might be preferred. If the teacher wanted to give students detailed feedback about their performance on each particular evaluative criterion, she would use an analytic scoring guide.

No matter whether you want to assess student work holistically or analytically, all the important criteria identified in Step 1 should be incorporated into the scoring guide. The difference is that the analytic approach would address each criterion separately, while a holistic approach requires the writing of a single description that integrates all of the criteria of student performance at each level.

An analytic rubric allows a student to perform poorly in one area and still receive an overall high grade. Since students earn points for several evaluative criteria, the loss of one point for an error in punctuation or capitalization will have a limited effect on the total score. In contrast, scoring with a holistic rubric may reduce the student's grade if the work has only one area that is weak, because all criteria are considered at once and any flaw has the potential to lower the overall judgment of the performance.

The rubric for the measurement task could be either holistic or analytic. We chose to use the analytic approach because there are a number of discrete skills to evaluate. For example, one student might use a reasonable scale but have inaccurate measurements, while another might select a scale that is too large but have correct measurements. In a holistic rubric both students might receive the same score, and the nature of the student difficulty would be lost.

If a holistic approach were appropriate, the next step would be to decide on the scale for the rubric, that is, how many levels it will include. This matter will be addressed in the discussion of Step 3.

The selection of an analytic approach to scoring rather than a holistic approach results in three possibilities for scoring guides. The checklist, point-allocated checklist, and analytic rubric are all analytic approaches. If the teacher simply wants a record of whether or not the student demonstrated a skill, then a checklist is appropriate. In using a checklist, the teacher need only put blanks in front of each criterion on the list to provide a place for indicating whether or not the performance was acceptable.

If it is important to recognize different levels of performance related to some criteria, a point-allocated checklist might be better. In the case of the measurement task, some of the evaluative criteria lend themselves to assessing performance at different levels. For example, in doing a floor plan, students would have to measure the size of the room as well as several pieces of furniture. They would also have to decide if they should use centimeters or meters or inches or feet or some combination of appropriate units. What level of perfection is needed to receive a check? Must the work be flawless? Would one measurement error mean the student gets no credit? What if the room dimensions were given in inches rather than feet? Would the failure to use the traditional combination of feet and inches for the units deny credit even if all the measurements were correct? Clearly, awarding more than one point for this dimension of performance would allow variation in the scores of a student whose work is flawless and a student who places an eight-foot sofa along a five-foot wall but does everything else correctly.

A point-allocated checklist can also weight certain criteria to show that some areas of performance are valued more than others. For example, in grading essays, if five points are allocated to evaluating mechanics and grammar and twenty points are allocated for the content, the implicit message is that mechanics and grammar are important, but content is of greater importance in light of the learning outcomes being assessed by the task. The same strategy of weighting criteria can be used in an analytic rubric.

The difference between a point-allocated checklist and a rubric is that a rubric explicitly defines levels of performance for each criterion. Based on an earlier discussion, you can see that a point-allocated checklist for the measurement task might give three points for the criterion "accurate measurement with appropriate units." As we discussed in the beginning of the chapter, an analytic rubric would explicitly communicate what is expected for a three-point response while a point-allocated checklist would not.

In determining which of the three types of scoring guides to use, the teacher must consider whether there is a need to define levels of performance explicitly. The scoring guide is finished if he is to use a checklist. For all other scoring guides, the next step involves decisions about selecting a scale for the guide.

Step 3. Develop rating scales for the scoring guide.

The *American Heritage Dictionary* offers one definition of *scale* that fits this discussion of rubrics: "A progressive classification, as of size, amount, importance, or rank." The formation of a point-allocated checklist requires the teacher to decide the number of points—the amount—to give each criterion. The decision about how to allocate points is an actual communication of the importance of each evaluative criterion. Thus, in grading a social studies report the teacher might allocate more points to criteria related to the content of the report and fewer points to form and format issues, such as grammar, mechanics, spelling, and neatness. But in an English class where students are writing historical fiction, more credit might be given to matters of writing style and less for the content.

In rubrics, numbers or categorical labels are used to designate the level of performance. Figure 4–4 used labels—Expert, Accomplished, Novice—rather than numbers to rank the performances demonstrated in students' limericks. It would have been just as appropriate to use numbers. In fact, the holistic rubric for mathematics communication in Figure 4–6 uses a combination of category names and numbers—Accomplished (3), Developing (2), Not Yet (1). Notice the larger the number, the more proficient the response.

The designation of a numerical scale that increases for higher levels of performance allows the teacher to combine the domains to get a single grade, as in an analytic rubric, or to use rubric scores from performance assessments in combination with scores from other types of assessment. We will discuss turning rubric scores into letter grades later in the chapter.

In selecting a scale, the teacher must determine how many levels of proficiency to define and decide what labels or numbers to associate with each level. The selection of evaluative criteria sometimes controls the number of levels in a scale because the teacher can only describe a limited number of performance levels for a particular criterion.

For example, the analytic rubric in Figure 4–3 has only two levels for scoring the number of lines criterion—the limerick either had five lines or it didn't. But it uses three levels for the evaluation of the other criteria, such as "contains descriptive words," because the teacher could define three levels of proficiency for them. Writing the descriptions that are to define the scale helps the teacher determine how many levels are appropriate for a given criterion.

In designing a rubric for the measurement task, the teacher would be able to define several levels for most of the evaluative criteria. Development of the descriptions usually begins with writing the narrative for the highest level of performance. The first step in writing the rubric in Figure 4–8 was to write a description for top performance on the criterion "Accurate measurement with appropriate units." In the development of this task-specific rubric, the evaluative criteria as well as the descriptors limit the use of the rubric to scale-drawing tasks. The descriptions of lower proficiency levels are based on what was written for the highest level. The lower levels are defined by how often students made measurement errors and their use of appropriate units. Using the language in the highest performance level to write the narrative for other levels helps the teacher create parallel structures for the descriptors for various levels of performance.

Four different descriptions could be written that clearly define unique levels of performance for most of the criteria. However, only three levels could be defined for the criteria "Neatness" and "Use of appropriate

Student Name: Date:

The Drawing	Level 1	Level 2	Level 3	Level 4
Accurate measurement with appropriate units	Many measurements have errors and inappropriate or missing units.	Some measurements have errors and inappropriate or missing units.	Some measurements have errors or inappropriate or missing units.	All measurements are correct and labeled with appropriate units.
Appropriate use of a reasonable scale	Drawing is not done to scale.	Only a few features in the drawing are correctly scaled.	Most features in the drawing are correctly scaled.	All features of the drawing are correctly scaled.
Appropriate form showing title, scale key, labels, architectural notations	Many required elements of the drawing contain errors and some are missing.	Some required elements of the drawing contain errors and some are missing.	Some required elements of the drawing contain errors or some are missing.	All required elements of the drawing are present and correct.
Neatness	Lines, printing, and finished product are not done neatly.	Lines, printing, or finished product are not done neatly.	Lines, printing, and finished product are done neatly.	

The Presentation	Level 1	Level 2	Level 3	Level 4
Use of appropriate measurement terms	Terms are used incorrectly or units not mentioned.	Some terms are used correctly.	All terms are used correctly.	
Accurate description of the measurements of 5 features in the drawing	Descriptions of measurements are not given or are incorrect.	Measurements of 1 or 2 features in the drawing are accurately described.	Measurements of 3 or 4 features in the drawing are accurately described.	Measurements of 5 or more features in the drawing are accurately described.

FIGURE 4–8   *Analytic rubric for measurement task*

measurement terms." When the criteria in a rubric result in the use of a different number of levels for some criteria, those that have the higher number of levels are of course worth more points. These criteria, therefore, have a greater weight in determining the final grade. The teacher must consider if this effect on the final grade is appropriate. In our example, neatness will be only a three-point consideration in the grade on the scale drawing, while other criteria will count for four points.

If the number of levels in a rubric must be determined by the number of descriptions a teacher can write, it is important to consider what makes a good descriptor. Descriptors should:

1. address quantitative and/or qualitative aspects of the criterion
2. address the same elements of performance at each level
3. avoid generic adjectives such as *good, poor, weak*, and *excellent*
4. try to suggest needed improvements rather than noting deficiencies

First, the teacher must think about the quantitative and qualitative characteristics of performance that she will consider in grading the work. For example, in writing a persuasive letter, the author might be expected to give at least a certain number of reasons to support a point of view. The rubric might say, "At least three different reasons are given." On the other hand, in a fictional narrative, a teacher may not want to count the number of adjectives in the piece at all. Thus, as in Figure 4–9, the descriptor might focus on qualitative characteristics: "Vivid descriptions are used effectively in some parts of the narrative." In this example a quantitative consideration is also incorporated when the difference between the top two levels refers to frequency, using the phrases "throughout the narrative" in Level 4 and "in some parts of the narrative" in Level 3.

In mathematics a quantitative descriptor may focus on the number of computation errors to determine whether a paper is at one level or another. In other cases, the variation may be related to such qualitative elements as how organized, clear, or thorough the response is. A student's response to a

Levels	Descriptors
4	Vivid descriptions of people, places, and emotions are used effectively throughout the narrative.
3	Vivid descriptions are used effectively in some parts of the narrative.
2	Attempts to use descriptions, but use of descriptive words is awkward or inappropriate.
1	Needs descriptive language.

FIGURE 4–9 *Levels of performance for use of descriptive words*

problem-solving task may be judged at a higher level because the explanation of strategies used is thorough, clearly illustrated, or well organized.

As mentioned earlier, use of parallel structures by addressing the same elements of performance in the descriptions at each level enhances the clarity of the language in a rubric. For example, the first criterion in the rubric for the measurement task (Figure 4–8) addresses both accuracy of measurements and use of unit labels at all four proficiency levels. At the lowest level, student work contains many measurement errors and unit labels are not appropriate, while at the highest level all measurements are correct and appropriately labeled. In a similar manner, the descriptor at each level of the first criterion addresses both accuracy of measurement and labeling.

In a holistic rubric several evaluative criteria are considered simultaneously and a change between proficiency levels may be triggered by variation in only one criterion. It is better to repeat the descriptions of the unchanged elements rather than to ignore them. The holistic scoring guide in Figure 4–10 illustrates this strategy. The descriptions of Levels 4, 5, and 6 include the statement "Lines, printing, and the finished product are done neatly." Other elements of performance define the difference between an adequate and an outstanding response.

Also notice that the holistic rubric for the measurement task has six levels while the analytic rubric has only three or four levels for each criterion. More levels are needed in the holistic case because many different types of student performances must be considered in combination to select the score. Without a larger number of levels, it would be very difficult to decide what score a student should receive if he meets one performance expectation for a level for one criterion but does not meet another. Some teachers might use the same four-level schema for both the holistic and analytic rubrics and augment the scale by using plus and minus, similar to letter grading schema used in report cards, that is A+, A, A–, and so on).

When the description of a proficiency level involves more than one element, the use of *and* and *or* can distinguish between levels. Such is the case for the evaluative criterion "Tells a funny story" in the analytic rubric for scoring limericks (Figure 4–3). This criterion implied that the limerick both told a complete story and was funny. A limerick of high quality would be characterized by both elements. In defining the next lowest level of performance, the teacher might want to recognize that a limerick could be humorous but not tell a complete story, or it might tell a story that is not funny. Thus on a three-point rubric, the middle level of performance reads, "The story that the limerick tells is incomplete *or* is not funny." The lowest level reads, "The story that the limerick tells is incomplete *and* is not funny." Both the analytic and holistic rubrics for the measurement task make use of the conjunctions *and* and *or* to distinguish levels of proficiency.

The third characteristic of clear rubric descriptions emphasizes the importance of providing details in descriptors. The measurement rubric avoids the use of *good, weak,* and *poor* by providing specific descriptions of what the teacher expects to see in student work. The use of such words as *excellent* and *poor* fails to provide details that communicate what is expected to be

LEVELS	DESCRIPTORS
Level 6	All measurements are correct and labeled with appropriate units. All features of the drawing are correctly scaled, and all required elements of the drawing are present and correct. Lines, printing, and the finished product are done neatly. In the presentation, all terms were used correctly and the student accurately described the measurements of 5 or more features in the drawing.
Level 5	The student work is characterized by most of the following statements. There are some errors in measurements or inappropriate or missing units. All features of the drawing are correctly scaled, but some required elements contain errors and some are missing. Lines, printing, and the finished product are done neatly. In the presentation, all terms were used correctly and the student accurately described the measurements of only 3 or 4 features in the drawing.
Level 4	The student work is characterized by most of the following statements. There are some errors in measurements or inappropriate or missing units. Most features in the drawing are correctly scaled, but some required elements contain errors and some are missing. Lines, printing, and the finished product are done neatly. In the presentation, most terms were used correctly and the student accurately described the measurements of only 3 or 4 features in the drawing.
Level 3	The student work is characterized by most of the following statements. There are some errors in measurements and inappropriate or missing units. Most features in the drawing are correctly scaled, and some required elements contain errors while others are missing. Lines, printing, or finished product are not done neatly. In the presentation, only some terms were used correctly and the student accurately described the measurements of only 1 or 2 features in the drawing.
Level 2	The student work is characterized by most of the following statements. There are some errors in measurements and inappropriate or missing units. Only a few features in the drawing are correctly scaled, and some required elements contain errors while others are missing. Lines, printing, or finished product are not done neatly. In the presentation, only some terms were used correctly and the student accurately described the measurements of only 1 or 2 features in the drawing.
Level 1	There are many errors in measurements and inappropriate or missing units. The drawing is not done to scale, and many required elements contain errors and some are missing. Lines, printing, and finished product are not done neatly. In the presentation, terms were used incorrectly or units were not mentioned. The descriptions of measurements were not given or were incorrect.

Student Name: Date:

FIGURE 4–10   *Holistic rubric for measurement task*

achieved at a specific level. The labeling of a piece of work as *good* is subject to interpretation and confusion.

Why is *good* not good enough? Imagine substituting the descriptions *poor, good,* and *excellent* in the analytic rubric for limericks given earlier. The comparison of the original and new descriptions is provided in Figure 4–11. Students receiving a "Good" would not learn how to write a better piece. They may not understand that specific nouns, adjectives, and adverbs make the difference between an excellent and good performance. They may have seen their use of several adjectives as providing excellent descriptions and not realize that they also need to use adverbs or nouns to strengthen their limerick. The use of such general descriptors keeps the expectations for performance a secret.

A final consideration in writing descriptors is the use of language that is supportive of student learning by suggesting what the child needs to do rather than noting what is missing. For example, in Figure 4–4 the descriptors at the lowest level suggest "the limerick needs to contain specific nouns, adjectives, and adverbs" instead of saying "the limerick does not contain specific nouns, adjectives, and adverbs." Sometimes attempts to use such language result in descriptions that seem unclear or unnecessarily awkward. The decision about language should be guided by consideration of which approach more clearly communicates expectations to students.

Contains descriptive words (Distinct language from from Figure 4–3)	**1** No use of specific nouns, adjectives, and adverbs to paint a picture for the reader.	**2** Attempt to select specific nouns, adjectives, and adverbs to paint a picture for the reader.	**3** Effective selection of specific nouns, adjectives, and adverbs to paint a picture for the reader.

Or

Contains descriptive words (Less effective substitution of generic language in descriptors)	**1** Poor	**2** Good	**3** Excellent

FIGURE 4–11   *Comparison of language in descriptors*

RUBRIC SCORES AND STUDENT GRADES

The use of scoring guides often results in students asking, "What score do I need to get an A?" Families may also find rubric scores incomprehensible and want to know what they mean. In such cases, the teacher must be prepared to explain what rubric scores mean based on traditional indicators of student learning, such as letter grades.

Scores assigned with the rubrics and checklists discussed in this chapter can easily be associated with letter grades. Using the holistic rubric for limericks (Figure 4–4), the teacher may decide that a student earns a grade of C if the response is at the Novice level, a grade of B at the Accomplished level, and a grade of A at the Expert level.

When using an analytic rubric, the teacher can determine a grade by adding the scores for the evaluative criteria and then designating a letter grade for a certain span of scores. For example, in the analytic rubric for the measurement task (Figure 4–8), the highest possible total score would be 22—four criteria with a high score of 4 and two criteria with a high score of 3. A teacher might decide that scores of 19 to 22 will be A's, scores of 16 to 18 will be B's, and so on. There is no single right way to make such conversions. It's just important that the teacher communicates to students and their families the meaning of scores in terms of the expected standards of performance and grades.

SPECIAL CONSIDERATIONS

The design of a scoring guide should take into account differences in learners. The ages of students and their language fluency, for example, are considerations. When scoring guides are used with pre- or emergent readers, teachers sometimes use pictures instead of words or numbers to represent the concepts to be learned. To introduce children to scoring guides, it is probably best to use checklists at first and then move toward rubrics, because the use of scales and weights in creating scoring guides could be confusing to young learners.

For example, a checklist for four- or five-year-olds who are learning about directions such as right, left, up, and down might use an icon approach as shown in Figure 4–12. Notice that the use of words and icons will help the child and family communicate about what has been learned.

Other icon-based checklists could be used to show skills such as using scissors (✄), knowing a phone number (☎) or address (✉), and using a computer keyboard (⌨) or the mouse (🖱). Imaginative use of clip art and computer fonts makes it possible for teachers to create icon-based scoring guides for young learners. The teacher will, of course, have to explain the significance of the symbols and what the check means when first using such checklists.

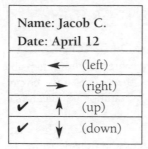

Name: Jacob C. Date: April 12		
	←	(left)
	→	(right)
✔	↑	(up)
✔	↓	(down)

FIGURE 4–12   *Icon-based checklist*

Once students become familiar with checklists, teachers may want to begin using an icon-based rubric that will communicate variation in levels of performance. Figure 4–13 uses multiple stars to indicate a greater level of proficiency with counting. The specific skills relate to knowing counting words, knowing symbols, and being able to count collections of objects. Notice that the use of both symbols and words results in a scoring guide that can be interpreted by both children and adults.

POWER OF RUBRICS AND CHECKLISTS

The types of scoring guides described in this chapter do much to enhance the teaching and learning environment. As we mentioned earlier, teachers have an easier time evaluating student work and being fair in their evaluation when using a well-constructed scoring guide. At the same time, the use of rubrics and checklists supports student learning. Students develop a clear understanding of what is expected if they receive both the task directions and the evaluation rubric at the same time. The rubric serves to direct stu-

NAME: Avery C.		Date: Oct. 15, 2000	
Knows counting words	★ "one" to "five"	★★ "one" to "ten"	★★★ "one" to "fifteen"
Knows symbols	★ 1, 2, 3, 4, 5	★★ 1, 2, 3, …, 10	★★★ 1, 2, 3, …, 15
Counts objects	★ up to 5	★★ up to 10	★★★ up to 15

FIGURE 4–13   *Icon-based rubric*

dent attention to the important concepts and skills they should demonstrate in completing the task. Such open communication with students can serve to reduce anxiety. Further, the teacher-student relationship during assessment is changed from an adversarial one to a pedagogical one. The assessment is not an occasion for the teacher to catch the student in an error, but an opportunity for students to demonstrate what they have learned.

5 | SELECTED-RESPONSE ITEMS

Any item that requires the student to select an answer from a set of choices is referred to as a selected-response item. Please note the use of the term *item*. An item is basically a test question. However, all test items are not presented in the form of a question, so referring to them as questions is inaccurate. The more general term *item* takes care of that discrepancy. Multiple-choice items typically have four or five choices, called alternatives, though, as you will see in Figure 5–1, some items offer only three choices.

Standard: Predict the results of actions based on data and experiences. The student will investigate and understand temperature scales, heat, and heat transfer. Key concepts include applications of heat transfer. (South Carolina Curriculum Standards)

Note that question 34 has only three choices.

34 The diagram at the right shows an activity in which a large open can full of air is placed on a balance. The can is removed, heated, and placed on the balance again. Which diagram below shows how the balance most likely will look just after the can is heated?

 A.    B.   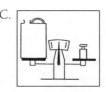 C.

FIGURE 5–1   *Multiple-choice science item*

Other examples of selected-response items are true-false and matching. True-false items have only two choices, while matching items have several. The main defining characteristic of a selected-response item is that the answer is one of the choices given with the item, unlike a performance assessment for which students must construct a response. For selected-response items, a student merely has to select the correct answer from the alternatives presented, but, as many students will attest, that is not always as easy as it sounds.

This chapter focuses on the characteristics and use of selected-response items. We will discuss separately the purpose and power of multiple-choice, true-false, and matching items. Then, we will provide some suggestions for how to make sense of student performance with selected-response items.

MULTIPLE-CHOICE ITEMS

Purpose and power of multiple-choice items

Multiple-choice tests became popular in the 1970s as more and more states began implementing required assessment programs. Using multiple-choice items allows one to quickly assess the learning of a broad array of concepts. Scoring of such tests involves only verifying that the correct alternative was selected. There is no student writing to interpret or partial credit to award, as would be the case with an essay-type question. Through the use of an answer form on which students fill in bubbles to indicate their answer selections, multiple-choice items can be scored using computers, making the scoring process even quicker. For these reasons, multiple-choice test items can be useful when there is a need to assess the learning of a large number of students.

The use of multiple-choice items is sometimes characterized as limiting the scope of learning that can be assessed. However, this view is based on a fallacy that multiple-choice items can assess only the recall of facts. While many multiple-choice items are written to do just that, it is possible to assess higher levels on Bloom's Taxonomy such as application of knowledge and even analysis, synthesis, and evaluation. For example, Figure 5–1 shows a synthesis question in which students must apply what they have learned by integrating science content knowledge with process skills.

In the situation described in Figure 5–1, initially, the can has the same mass as the object shown on the right of the scale (see the original picture). When the can is heated, the air inside expands, forcing some of the air out of the can and leaving less air inside. As a result, the mass of the air in the can is less. When this heated can containing less air is again placed on the balance, its total mass will be less than it originally was and less than the mass of object on the right. This will cause the balance to tilt as shown in choice A., the correct answer.

This question is a typical multiple-choice item commonly found on classroom, school, district, state, and national tests. To correctly answer the item, students must understand the text of the question, interpret the diagram, and then select the best answer to the question from three choices.

For this multiple-choice question, students must have content knowledge as well as predict the results of an experiment. Science test items often involve the integration of content knowledge with science process skills, that is, skills used to obtain and understand scientific information. The science process skills include observation, inference, classification, measurement, prediction, experimentation, and communication. The examples that follow further illustrate various levels of learning assessed by multiple-choice items.

This third-grade test item is at the knowledge level of Bloom's Taxonomy:

The Earth makes one revolution around the Sun in one
  A. day.
  B. month.
  C. week.
  D. year.

Students are taught that it takes one year for the Earth to revolve around the Sun. Third graders would be expected to know the meaning of the word *revolution*. To answer the item, they simply have to recall or recognize the information they were taught. For this test item, they must select the best answer from four alternatives. The correct answer is choice D, year.

The question for middle schoolers in Figure 5–2 is more complicated. Middle school students have studied the geography and history of various

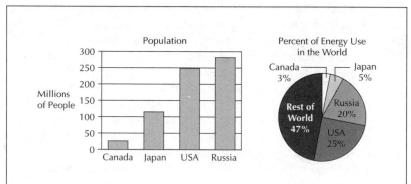

Which conclusion is most likely based on the graphs?

A. The more people in a country, the more energy the country uses.
B. The more people in a country, the less energy the country uses.
C. The country using the most energy does not have the largest population.
D. Energy use has nothing to do with the number of people in a country.

FIGURE 5–2   *Multiple-choice social studies item*

countries. To answer this question they must analyze two sources of information, a pie chart (circle graph) that shows the countries that use the most energy and a bar graph that shows the number of people in those same countries.

First, the students must analyze two separate graphs, which involves applying skills learned in mathematics class. The bar graph shows the population of four countries. The energy use for those four countries and the rest of the world is represented by the pie chart. The students must synthesize this information along with the content they have been taught about how countries, particularly industrialized nations, use energy. Then they must draw a reasonable conclusion about the relationship between energy use and population. Students should know that, generally, there is greater energy use per person in industrialized nations. Based on this content information and the information shown in the graph, it is reasonable to conclude that choice C is correct. Please note that this is the only valid conclusion out of the four alternatives given based on the information presented. However, other conclusions are also possible; they're just not listed as alternatives.

One of the advantages of multiple-choice items is that the answer choices are restricted to those provided. As a result, less is open to interpretation by the students. However, the choices also limit the possible responses, as indicated in Figure 5–2. One of the drawbacks to multiple-choice items is that they can lead to guessing. No matter how well written or how complicated they are, students always have a chance to get the items right. Students are able to get some items correct by eliminating one or two choices and guessing among the remaining alternatives. By carefully constructing multiple-choice items, test designers can reduce the chances of students guessing correctly. Scores will then more accurately show what the students know, but the effect of guessing will never be completely eliminated.

Figure 5–3 illustrates an item that requires the application of knowledge to solve a problem. During a lesson, students work with spinners and are taught about the probability of landing on each section of the spinner. To answer the question in Figure 5–3, they must apply their knowledge of probability and their experience with spinners in a new context to demonstrate their understanding. The data in the table indicate that the pointer lands on the shuttle half the time and on the sailboat one-third of the time. As shown by spinner A, the correct answer, the shuttle portion is 50 percent or half of the spinner. The sailboat takes up one-third (33.3 percent) of the spinner, the balloon takes up one-tenth (10 percent), and the helicopter one-fifteenth (6.7 percent).

Just as students' experience with spinners helps them to better understand this test item, experience with multiple-choice items helps students better understand how to answer that type of item. As with all types of test items, students need to be familiar with the format. Each item format requires students to use their knowledge and skills a little differently. For example, in the case of a multiple-choice item, the correct answer is included

Katie spun the pointer on a spinner 150 times and put the results in this table.

Picture				
Number of times pointer landed on the picture	75	50	15	10

Which spinner did Katie most likely use?

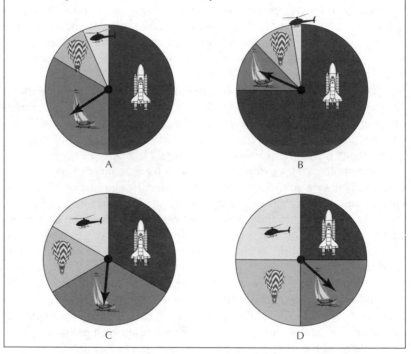

FIGURE 5–3   *Multiple-choice mathematics item*

as one of the alternatives. The teacher expects each student to choose among the given alternatives. A student who lacks knowledge and doesn't guess is at a disadvantage since that student will automatically get the item wrong, while peers who are more experienced with the multiple-choice format are more likely to guess in the same situation, giving them a chance to get the item correct.

Some multiple-choice items require students to select the "best alternative" from among the choices presented. When this type of item is presented the choices may contain several plausible alternatives, but one of these is considered the best choice in light of the situation presented in the item. Students who have not had experience distinguishing between specific alternatives may find this type of test item difficult to answer. For example, a mathematics test item might ask a student to choose the term that *best* describes a child's building block. The choices might be: (A.) cube, (B.) polyhedron, (C.) prism, and (D.) square. Alternative D would be an incorrect answer because *square* is a term for a two-dimensional shape. All three of the other choices are plausible. A child's block is a cube, a special kind of polyhedron, and a (rectangular) prism. However, the term *cube* provides the most information and the most accurate description. Thus, choice A is the best answer.

Teachers may wonder how many alternatives to provide in a multiple-choice item. Most of the multiple-choice items discussed so far have four alternatives, which is typical. A few, such as the one in Figure 5–1 and Revision 2 (see "Guideline 2") have only three choices that cover all reasonable alternatives. On some assessments, five alternatives are provided, which makes an item more difficult by making it less likely the student will be able to guess correctly. The number of plausible alternatives that can be written should guide the number of choices in the item. We recommend that teachers limit the number of alternatives to four for students in elementary and middle school, possibly increasing to five alternatives in grade 8 and high school.

Throughout this section, multiple-choice items will be shown with alternatives labeled A through D. We have chosen this format though other acceptable formats could also be used. Some teachers may prefer lowercase letters; others prefer numbers, though these can be confusing in math or science items when the choices themselves include numbers. Also, because numbers are typically used to label items, letters are better for labeling choices in the items.

Effective multiple-choice items

Good multiple-choice items are not easy to write. However, the quick and efficient scoring of student papers offsets the time invested in developing good items. Each multiple-choice item begins with a stem—the question or statement that sets up the problem. The stem is followed by several choices or alternatives. The incorrect choices are referred to as distractors.

There are several common problems that writers encounter when developing multiple-choice items. Testing staff at the New York State Education Department have a list of points to consider while developing a test item (NYSED 1989). Similar lists of do's and don'ts are cited by Haladyna (1997), Airasian (1997), Popham (1978), and Osterlind (1998), to name just a few. (Many different authors have developed guidelines for writing test items. A variety of sources have been consulted and may be helpful to the reader. It is not the intent of the authors to slight anyone who may have similar guidelines.) The following list contains guidelines associated with writing multiple-choice items. Each of the points will be addressed in detail in the following discussions.

Guidelines for Writing Effective Multiple-Choice Test Items

1. Write items in clear and simple language, keeping vocabulary as simple as possible.
2. Base each item on a single central idea that is stated clearly and completely in the stem.
3. Use either a direct question or an incomplete statement for the stem.
4. Include in the stem words that would be repeated in all alternatives.
5. Avoid negative wording in the stem.
6. Avoid "window dressing" in the stem.
7. Avoid providing clues to the correct alternative.
8. Place alternatives at the end of an incomplete statement.
9. Write alternatives that are grammatically consistent with the stem and parallel to one another in form.
10. Use alternatives that are plausible to students who lack the knowledge and/or skills tested by the item.
11. Make alternatives independent and mutually exclusive.
12. Use alternatives that are approximately the same length.
13. Arrange alternatives in logical order, if one exists.
14. Avoid using "none of these" and "all of the above" as alternatives.
15. List alternatives either vertically or horizontally.
16. Verify that each item has one and only one correct answer.

When writing test items, there is one fundamental guiding principle: when a student answers a question incorrectly, it should be because he lacks the information or skills necessary to correctly answer the question, not because the structure of the question leads the student to an incorrect response. If testing is to be valid, there can be no trick questions. When students respond incorrectly because of structural problems with an item, the question does not contribute information about what the student knows or is able to do. The following examples illustrate the sixteen guidelines previously listed. For each example, we provide a sample question and suggest a revision. We also provide an explanation of how the revision strengthens the question. The section of the item that should be revised is shown in italics in each example.

Guideline 1: Write items in clear and simple language, keeping vocabulary as simple as possible.

Example 1

Joe is planning to construct *an edifice. The longest wall of the edifice will be 50 meters long. On one end of this wall and perpendicular to it,* a wall that is 25 meters long will be constructed. On the other end, a 35-meter long wall will be constructed also perpendicular to it. Perpendicular to the other end of the 25-meter wall, a 40-meter wall will be constructed toward the 35-meter wall. Perpendicular to the other end of the 35-meter wall will be a 10-meter wall built in the direction of the 25-meter wall. Then, a short wall will be built perpendicular to both the 10-meter and the 40-meter wall to connect them and close the building. What is the area of the building?

A. 160 square meters
B. 170 square meters
C. 1350 square meters
D. 1750 square meters

Revision 1

Joe is planning to construct a building with the dimensions shown in the diagram.

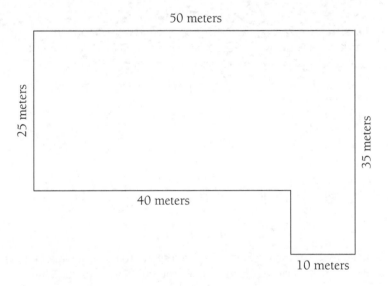

What is the area of the building?

A. 160 square meters
B. 170 square meters
C. 1350 square meters
D. 1750 square meters

The purpose of this question is to test whether students can find the area of a shape, not to assess their knowledge of vocabulary or their reading ability. The original version of this question provides lots of written details that are difficult to follow. The question is clearer when a diagram is used instead of the wordy description of the building.

Reading level, also referred to as "reading load," is an important consideration when constructing items in subjects such as mathematics and science. If the reading load of an item is high, poor readers will have trouble understanding what the item is asking. Unless the item is intended to assess reading ability, teachers should try to keep the reading level as low as possible. Similarly, unless the item is intended to test vocabulary, the words should be as simple as possible. For example, many students may not know the word *edifice* and some will assume they can't do the mathematics problem because they don't know the meaning of this word. Substituting the word *building* actually conveys more meaning to the typical student, who can now visualize the problem in terms of her or his real-world experiences.

Guideline 2: Base each item on a single central idea that is stated clearly and completely in the stem.

Example 2

Refer to the graphs in Figure 5–2 to respond to the following item. *Based on the graphs, how does the population and energy use of the United States compare to the population and energy use of Japan?*

    A. *The United States uses more energy and has a larger population than Japan.*

    B. *The United States uses more energy and has a smaller population than Japan.*

    C. *The United States uses less energy and has a smaller population than Japan.*

    D. *The United States uses the same amount of energy and has the same size population as Japan.*

Revision 2

Refer to the graphs in Figure 5–2 to respond to the following item. Based on the bar graph, how does the population of the United States compare to the population of Japan?

    A. The United States has more people than Japan.
    B. The United States has fewer people than Japan.
    C. The United States has the same number of people as Japan.

According to the pie chart, how does the energy use in the United States compare to the energy use in Japan?

    A. The United States uses more energy than Japan.
    B. The United States uses less energy than Japan.
    C. The United States uses the same amount of energy as Japan.

Example 2 asks two different questions: which country uses more energy and which country has the larger population. Students are required to interpret the two graphs independently. As a result, the four alternatives are very long, increasing the reading load of the item, and students must sort through two sets of information in order to respond to the question. For students who answer incorrectly, the teacher will not know if they have trouble interpreting one graph or both.

Revision 2 shows the single question divided into two separate items, each one focused on a different central idea. For each item in the revision, students must analyze one graph. If the items were separated on a test, the teacher would not have to indicate the type of graph—bar graph or pie chart—in the stem. The revised items only have three plausible alternatives. When an item requires a response format of "more, less, or the same"—or "increase, decrease, or remain the same"—it is important that the three alternatives are listed in the same order for each similar item so students are not tricked by one item having "increase" as alternative A and another item having "increase" as alternative B.

Note that Example 2 is very different from the item in Figure 5–2. Example 2 includes two central ideas, each of which can be asked more clearly as a single item. Figure 5–2 contains a single central idea: the relationship between population and energy consumption.

Guideline 3: Use either a direct question or an incomplete statement for the stem.

Example 3: Incomplete Statement Format

Elena went to the store and spent $8.74, tax included. The combination of money that she could have used to pay is

    A. one $5 bill, three $1 bills, and 3 quarters.
    B. one $5 bill, three $1 bills, and 12 nickels.
    C. eight $1 bills and 1 quarter.
    D. eight $1 bills and 4 dimes.

Example 3: Direct Question Format

Elena went to the store and spent $8.74, tax included. Which combination of money could she have used to pay?

    A. one $5 bill, three $1 bills, and 3 quarters
    B. one $5 bill, three $1 bills, and 12 nickels
    C. eight $1 bills and 1 quarter
    D. eight $1 bills and 4 dimes

The writer must decide which of these formats is more appropriate, and that decision will depend on the specific item. A teacher could probably use either format in this case, but in some situations one form or the other might be easier for students to interpret.

Sometimes, the necessary structure for an incomplete statement is awkward and confusing to students. For example, if the question in Revision 2 was rewritten as an incomplete statement, it would read, "Compared to Japan, the United States has. . . ." Students would have no idea what the item was asking until they read the four alternatives, since the central idea is not completed in the stem (see Guideline 2). Alternatively, the item could be revised to read, "Compared to the population of Japan, the population of the United States is. . . ." Certainly this revision is shorter, to the point, and grammatically correct. In high school this sentence construction should be fine, but younger readers will find an item that begins with "compared to" very difficult to follow. In this case, the direct question is easier for the student to understand.

There are differences of opinion about the exact format for an item written in the incomplete statement format. Some writers put a blank line at the end of the statement and place a period after it. Others do not include the blank, but put periods at the end of each alternative to show that the alternative has completed the statement. Still others do not use the blank line or place a period at the end of the alternatives. The choice for formatting is yours. Just be consistent throughout your test so that students don't think there is a trick to how the item is formatted.

Guideline 4: Include in the stem words that would be repeated in all alternatives.

Example 4

One similarity between the U.S. House of Representatives and the U.S. Senate is that

    A. *both representatives and senators* are elected by the people.
    B. *both representatives and senators* are appointed by the president.
    C. *both representatives and senators* have terms that are six years long.
    D. *both representatives and senators* may serve for only two terms.

Revision 4

One similarity between the U.S. House of Representatives and the U.S. Senate is that both representatives and senators

    A. are elected by the people.
    B. are appointed by the president.
    C. have terms that are six years long.
    D. may serve for only two terms.

When words are repeated in each alternative, the test item becomes longer than necessary and more confusing to the student. If you put the repeated words into the stem, students only have to read them once, and the alternatives are shorter and clearer.

Read the story and then answer the question that follows.

Bowled Over

Jackie and her mom worked together quietly. They were finishing up the laundry: folding T-shirts and towels and rolling up pairs of socks. Nobody was talking. Finally, as they put away the last washcloth, Jackie asked the question that had been wanting to jump out of her mouth all night. "Mom, can I have a birthday party?"

"Umm, a birthday party. Were you thinking about a real party with balloons and pin the tail on the donkey and a special cake? Do you want me to make one with roses? Should we have a clown? Uncle Harry has a clown costume, you know."

Jackie rolled her eyes, but didn't let her mom see. To herself she wailed, "Oh, Mom!" But out loud she answered in her most polite, almost-ten-year-old voice, "Those ideas sound great, Mom, but I was thinking about something else. I really want a bowling party."

"A bowling party? What gave you that idea? Have you ever been bowling, Jackie?"

"No, I never have, and that's why I like the idea, Mom. I'm growing up, you know, and I want to try new things. I've heard other kids talking about how much fun bowling parties are. And the bowling places have package deals. You get to invite some friends and bowl and get hot dogs and even a neat cake if you want one. But your cake with the roses would be good, too."

"Well . . . I'll have to think about this. Bowling parties are all new to me, and they sound expensive. Besides, it's late. I'll check this out, and we'll see."

Example 5

Which event *did not happen* in the story?

    A. Jackie and her mother folded clothes.
    B. Jackie went bowling with her mother.
    C. Jackie's mother offered to make a birthday cake.
    D. Jackie explained why she wanted a bowling party.

Revision 5

Which event happened in the story?

    A. Jackie and her mother folded clothes.
    B. Jackie went bowling with her mother.
    C. Jackie's mother said Jackie couldn't have a bowling party.
    D. Jackie told her mother she didn't want a clown at her party.

When a student reads the question in Example 5, he must first recognize that the questions asks "Which *did not* happen?" and then he must go about the task of eliminating events that did occur in the story. Approaching the item from the negative perspective is more challenging to some students. Many students will simply miss the *not* and choose the first event in the list that occurred in the story (alternative A). When students misread items like this, it merely confirms what we already know: that students frequently miss negatively phrased items. As a result, teachers learn little about what students really know. If possible, phrase items positively, as shown in Revision 5; note that two alternatives had to be changed so that there is only one correct answer. If an item is phrased negatively, and some items are best written this way, then highlight the negative word. For example, underline or italicize the word *not*, as shown in Example 5.

Guideline 6: Avoid "window dressing" in the stem.

Example 6A

There are four different toppings that can be put on pizza. *The four toppings are pepperoni, olives, sausage, and peppers. These toppings can be combined in many different ways.* How many pizzas with 2 different toppings can be made?

  A. 1   B. 2   C. 6   D. 12

Revision 6A

There are four different toppings that can be put on pizza. How many pizzas with 2 different toppings can be made?

  A. 1   B. 2   C. 6   D. 12

Notice how long the example is. As shown in the revision, the question can be asked without the middle two sentences. The revised form of the question may not be as interesting, but it is much clearer, and students with less reading ability will find it easier to discern what is being asked here.

Teachers are trying to make their subjects more meaningful for students by tying the subject matter to the real world. This is especially true in mathematics. Real-world problems tend to contain more details than contrived problems that have little meaning other than as academic exercises. The idea is to use the examples to foster student interest but avoid unnecessary details that complicate the item. In Revision 6A, the item still incorporates the real-world application of pizza, but unnecessary details such as the names of the toppings—that is, the window dressing—have been avoided.

Be careful, however, that a complex problem is not oversimplified by removing important information. To assess understanding of a concept, it is often necessary to include additional information to determine if students are able to sort through several details and find the pertinent information. Example 6B illustrates this point.

Example 6B

Look at the triangle below.

What is the area of the triangle?

    A. 96 square inches
    B. *160 square inches*
    C. 192 square inches
    D. *240 square inches*

Oversimplification 6B

Look at the triangle below.

What is the area of the triangle?

    A. 20 square inches
    B. 96 square inches
    C. 192 square inches
    D. 384 square inches

For Example 6B, students must know how to find the area of a triangle—apply the formula $\frac{1}{2}(b \times h)$—and must determine which measurement is the height (h = 16 inches) and which measurement is the base (b = 24 inches). Students who are not really sure might use the 20 inches in calculating the area. Thus it is important for this measurement to be on the diagram, even though it is not used in the formula. The teacher will know that students who answered D (probably using 20 instead of 16 in the formula) or B (using 20 instead of 24) do not know how to apply the formula properly. Students who chose 96 square inches probably know which measurements to use but made a common mathematical mistake—multiplying $\frac{1}{2}b$ by $\frac{1}{2}h$). If the teacher uses the oversimplified version of the problem, valuable information about student understanding is lost, since the students do not have to sort through the complicating factor of 20 inches.

Guideline 7: Avoid providing clues to the correct alternative.

Example 7A

Of the fruits listed below, the one that contains the highest amount of vitamin C is *an*

    A. *pear.*
    B. *orange.*
    C. *grape.*
    D. *potato.*

Revision 7A

Of the fruits listed below, the one that contains the highest amount of vitamin C is

    A. a pear.
    B. an orange.
    C. a grape.
    D. an apple.

There are several clues to the correct answer in Example 7A. First, the use of the word *an* at the end of the statement indicates that the answer begins with a vowel, and orange is the only alternative beginning with a vowel. Remember, students who do not know the answer look for clues. Also, many students will know that a potato is not a fruit, eliminating it as a possibility and reducing their choices to three. Notice that in Revision 7A, the clues have been addressed by removing *an* from the stem and putting *an* or *a* in the alternatives and making the fourth choice a fruit.

When using the incomplete statement format, it is natural to mentally complete the statement with the correct answer. Then, the task of selecting appropriate distractors begins. As illustrated in Example 7A, it is easy to overlook the inclusion of a clue to the correct answer. In that case a simple rewrite corrects the problem. Other clues to correct answers may not be so obvious, as illustrated in Example 7B. This example is a question that is connected to the earlier story about Jackie wanting a birthday party at the bowling alley.

Example 7B

According to the story, the package deal at the *bowling alley* includes

    A. a cake and a clown.
    B. bowling and hot dogs.
    C. hot dogs and something to drink.
    D. games and a cake with roses.

According to the story, the package deal Jackie tells her mother about includes

    A. a cake and a clown.
    B. bowling and hot dogs.
    C. hot dogs and something to drink.
    D. games and a cake with roses.

In Example 7B, referring to "the bowling alley" cues one answer. Students without any knowledge of the story may select the answer B because of the cue "bowling."

Sometimes one test item provides a clue for another, as illustrated in Example 7C. Here, the second item could help the student figure out the answer to the first. In Revision 7C, we have reworded the second item so that it no longer contains a clue to the first.

Example 7C

Which diagram illustrates a quadrilateral?

    A.

    B.

    C.

    D.

Another item appearing somewhere else in the test provides a clue:

The *quadrilateral* shown below is 4 meters long and 3 meters wide.

What is the perimeter of this *quadrilateral*?

    A. 7 meters
    B. 12 meters
    C. 14 meters
    D. 49 meters

Revision 7C

Which diagram illustrates a quadrilateral?

    A.

    B.

    C.

    D.

A revision of the other item appearing somewhere else in the test to remove the clue:

The *figure* shown below is 4 meters long and 3 meters wide.

What is the perimeter of this *figure*?
    A. 7 meters
    B. 12 meters
    C. 14 meters
    D. 49 meters

Imagine a student is stumped by the first item in Example 7C, so he takes a guess and moves on to the rest of the test. Then he happens upon the second item. There he finds the answer to the first item. In this case the student doesn't even need to know that a quadrilateral is any four-sided figure. The picture tells him loud and clear that the answer to the first item is A. A teacher can easily rewrite the perimeter item to avoid providing this clue, as Revision 7C shows.

Guideline 8: Place alternatives at the end of an incomplete statement.

Example 8

The _____ branch of government is where laws are made.
    A. executive
    B. judicial
    C. legislative

Revision 8

The branch of government where laws are made is the
    A. executive.
    B. judicial.
    C. legislative.

Again, think of the student who has difficulty reading. In Example 8, the student must stop and fill in the blank with each alternative as she reads through the list. It is easier to complete the sentence, as is required in Revision 8, as a student reads through the various alternatives. The revision reads more quickly and clearly.

Guideline 9: Write alternatives that are grammatically consistent with the stem and parallel to one another in form.

Example 9

The invention of the train benefited society by

    A. *eliminating the need for coal miners.*
    B. *it made long-distance travel faster.*
    C. *the improvement of working conditions for steelworkers.*
    D. *fewer settlers went to the western part of North America.*

Revision 9

The invention of the train benefited society by

    A. eliminating the need for coal miners.
    B. making long-distance travel faster.
    C. improving working conditions for steelworkers.
    D. bringing fewer settlers to the western part of North America.

As shown in Example 9, it is more difficult to read and understand the item when the alternatives are not grammatically consistent with the stem. Notice how you trip over alternative B, the correct answer, and probably pause to reread it. Alternative B is a complete sentence and does not appropriately complete the stem statement. The alternatives in the revision are grammatically consistent, causing the item to flow from the stem through each alternative.

Guideline 10: Use alternatives that are plausible to students who lack the knowledge and/or skills tested by the item.

Example 10A

There are four different toppings that can be put on pizza. How many pizzas with 2 different toppings can be made?

    A. *1*   B. *2*   C. *6*   D. *12*

Revision 10A

There are four different toppings that can be put on pizza. How many pizzas with 2 different toppings can be made?

    A. 2   B. 6   C. 8   D. 16

The answer to the pizza question in Example 10A is C, 6. But which distractors are plausible to students who do not know how to find the answer? It's possible that some students will choose 2 as the answer. A student might think that with four toppings, two go on one pizza and two go on the other, and conclude that there are two combinations. Some students may think that since two toppings go on each pizza and there are four different toppings, the problem is solved by multiplying 2×4. These students will get an answer of 8, so that is also a viable answer, though it is not one of the choices in Example 10A.

Are students likely to pick 1 or 12, or are these weak distractors? Neither of these numbers are the likely outcome of a common miscalculation by a student who is using the given numbers, nor is there a way of thinking about the problem that would lead one to say 1 or 12 is the answer. Keep in mind that the reason multiple-choice items have three or four distractors is to cut down on students guessing the correct answer. If students are not likely to choose two of the four answer choices, there are only two plausible alternatives and students have a 50 percent chance of guessing correctly. As a result, the teacher could not be sure that students who answered correctly really know how to do the problem.

In Revision 10A, the fourth distractor is 16. Is this a plausible alternative? Some students may key in on the 4 and, for lack of a better way, square the number. Since there is a mathematical way to get 16, it is more likely an unknowing student will choose it rather than 12. Teachers should review the incorrect answers students select. If teachers discover that no students select a particular distractor, they should reconsider that choice before using the item on another test.

In science, a good distractor is the science term that students always mix up with the correct answer, for example, *rotation* for *revolution*. In some cases using these types of distractors helps the science teacher identify a student's misconceptions about certain topics.

Example 10B

Which diagram shows the motion of the Sun, the Earth, and the Moon?

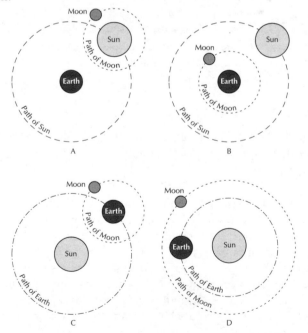

The correct answer to Example 10B is choice C. However, some students will select alternative B because they have the misconception that the Earth is at the center of the solar system. Some people avoid using these "obvious" distractors as a way to point test takers to the correct answer. But keep in mind, the purpose of the test is to find out what students know and can do and what they do not know and cannot do. Example 10B requires students to apply what they have learned. There are students who will say that the Sun is at the center of the solar system but will not conceptually understand that statement and choose a diagram that represents an Earth-centered solar system. Accurate information about students' knowledge and skills allows teachers to provide appropriate instruction to help their students learn better.

Guideline 11: Make alternatives independent and mutually exclusive.

Example 11A

Miguel had to carry 3 textbooks home (math, science, and social studies) to do his homework. He estimated the weight of the textbooks to be

    A. *more than 1 pound.*
    B. *more than 5 pounds.*
    C. *more than 10 pounds.*
    D. *more than 30 pounds.*

Revision 11A

Miguel had to carry 3 textbooks home (math, science, and social studies) to do his homework. He estimated the weight of the textbooks to be

    A. less than 1 pound.
    B. more than 1 pound, but less than 5 pounds.
    C. more than 5 pounds but less than 15 pounds.
    D. more than 15 pounds.

Let's say the three textbooks in Example 11A actually weigh twelve pounds. That means there are three correct answers to this item. As shown in Revision 11A, by providing ranges for weight, overlap in the alternatives is avoided. Teachers should keep in mind that textbook weight can vary greatly. If this type of item is to be used, then the details should be specific so that students can rely on their experience. As shown in the example, the three books are identified (this is not window dressing) so students using similar books would have an idea of how much they weigh. The problems in the following example are less obvious.

Read the passage to answer item 11B.

May 15, 1997

Dear Mom,

I know you are busy, so I want to help you know more about bowling parties. Last week I called the two bowling centers in town and asked them to send me some information about what kind of birthday party plans they have.

I found out that the best deal is at BOWL-A-RAMA. It's closer to our house, and it's cheaper too. The people at the bowling place do most of the work for the party. We can bowl for $1\frac{1}{2}$ hours and have another half hour for my party. We can have a soda and a hot dog to eat and my friends will get free game coupons and I will get a bowling pin. I hope it's a real one, and not a pin for my shirt, but I don't know.

The party will not cost too much. I want to invite the five friends in my Girl Scout group, and it costs only $5.00 for each person. That will just be $30.00 and we don't have to mess up the house and you don't have to work too hard to cook for us. I would like for you to make me a cake. Could it have bowling balls on it instead of roses?

I will help with my party, too. I will make the invitations and take them to my Scout meeting next Wednesday.

May I have a bowling party, please? I will always love you even if the answer is no.

Love,

Jackie

Example 11B

Choose the best answer. Based on Jackie's letter, the bowling center will give each of Jackie's friends

    A. *a hot dog.*

    B. *a hot dog and a soda.*

    C. *a hot dog, a soda, and free game coupons.*

    D. *a hot dog, a soda, free game coupons, and a bowling pin.*

Revision 11B–1

Based on Jackie's letter, the bowling center will give each of Jackie's friends

    A. 2 hours for each bowling game.

    B. a piece of cake with bowling balls.

    C. a hot dog and free bowling coupons.

    D. a bowling pin and a $5.00 coupon.

Because children will get a hot dog, soda, and game coupons at the party, three of the four choices in Example 11B are correct. The only incorrect answer is choice D, because only Jackie gets a bowling pin. Some writers use the term *best* as a cue to students that they must select the most complete choice as the "best" one. This is very confusing for students, especially elementary students, when items are written as Example 11B is. One revision would eliminate "hot dog" from three of the choices as seen in Revision 11B-1.

Some writers will eliminate the overlap by using a qualifier, such as the term *only*, to distinguish among the alternatives, as shown in Revision 11B-2. Using a qualifier is an acceptable way for dealing with this issue. However, this is still a difficult item structure for younger students. We suggest teachers write items in this format for older students only.

Revision 11B–2

Choose the best answer. Based on Jackie's letter, the bowling center will give each of Jackie's friends

    A. a hot dog, only.
    B. a hot dog and a soda, only.
    C. a hot dog, a soda, and free game coupons, only.
    D. a hot dog, a soda, free game coupons, and a bowling pin.

Guideline 12: Use alternatives that are approximately the same length.

Example 12A

Robert wants to work around his neighborhood during the summer to earn enough money to buy a bicycle. When talking to his neighbors about possible jobs he could do he should

    A. request a high salary.
    B. *request information regarding job responsibilities.*
    C. show little interest in the job.
    D. avoid asking questions.

Revision 12A

Robert wants to work around his neighborhood during the summer to earn enough money to buy a bicycle. When talking to his neighbors about possible jobs he could do he should

    A. request a high salary.
    B. ask about job responsibilities.
    C. show little interest in the job.
    D. avoid asking questions.

When students do not know the information being tested, they look for clues to the correct answer. One clue is an alternative that is very long or very short compared to the other alternatives, as shown in Example 12A.

The basic rule is that no alternative should stand out from the others. As shown in Revision 12A, the alternatives should be about the same length. Revision 11B-2 shows four alternatives that are all different lengths. In this case, none of the options stands out because it is the *only* long answer or the *only* short answer.

Example 12B

Refer to the letter for Example 11B to answer this item.

One reason Jackie gave her mother for having a bowling party was
   A. her friends could bowl all day.
   B. the party would only cost $30.00.
   C. she could have the party on Wednesday during her Scout meeting.
   D. the bowling place would mail the invitations to each of her friends.

Sometimes, it may not be possible to get all the alternatives the same length. When this happens, the teacher can present alternatives in pairs: two short and two long, as shown in Example 12B. When using five alternatives, it is a good idea to write three of one length and two of the other. A similar example showing alternatives paired by length is shown in Revision 11A. The alternatives are not grouped by length of statement, that is, two short followed by two long, because they are listed in order of increasing size, a guideline that will be discussed next.

Guideline 13: Arrange alternatives in logical order, if one exists.

Example 13A

All four solid objects shown below have the same mass. Which object is the most dense?

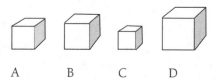

A   B   C   D

Revision 13A

All four solid objects shown below have the same mass. Which object is the most dense?

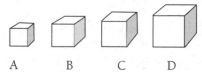

A   B   C   D

In Example 13A, the four solid objects should be arranged in order of size from smallest to largest, as shown in Revision 13A, or from largest to smallest. Doing so allows students to concentrate on determining the one with the greatest density without being distracted by trying to remember which object is bigger or smaller because the objects are not in order. Similarly, the alternatives in Revision 11A are listed in order of increasing weight.

Recall the discussion about plausible distractors under Guideline 10. In a question written like Example 13A, there are only two plausible alternatives: either the smallest or the biggest object has the greatest density if the mass of all objects is the same. In this example, the smallest object is the most dense.

Sometimes the logical order for the alternatives is guided by information in the test item, as in Example 13B.

Example 13B

Use the graph below to answer the question.

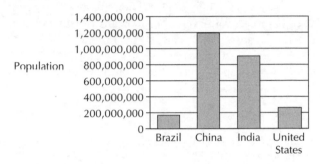

According to the graph, which nation has the largest population?

A. *Brazil*
B. *United States*
C. *India*
D. *China*

Revision 13B

According to the graph, which nation has the largest population?

A. Brazil
B. China
C. India
D. United States

For Revision 13B, the order of the countries is the same as the order shown on the graph. Following the same order makes it easier for the student to move between the graph and the alternatives. Please note that the countries are listed in alphabetical order, a common way to logically order terms and names in alternatives. Let's look at another example:

Example 13C

The square root of 9 is

   A. *1*   B. *3*   C. *9*   D. *81*

Revision 13C

The square root of 9 is

   A. 1   B. 9   C. 3   D. 81

In Example 13C, the alternatives have been placed in a logical order, increasing numerically. A similar situation occurred in Revision 10A. If the student only has to fill in a bubble preceding the alternative to indicate her answer, the logical order shown in Example 13C is fine. But what may happen if a student must record the answer on a separate answer sheet? The answer to this item is 3, option B. Some students may think "3" as they mark the third bubble on their answer sheet. Though the students calculated the answer correctly, they marked it wrong. In this case, the recommendation is to place any answer that is 1, 2, 3, 4, or 5 next to the corresponding letters A, B, C, D, or E, respectively, even when it means violating the logical order guideline. Thus, an answer of 3 would be next to the third letter, C.

Guideline 14: Avoid using "none of these" and "all of the above" as alternatives.

Example 14

Hilde cut a pie into 4 equal pieces and ate one of the pieces. How much of the pie is still left?

   A. $\frac{3}{4}$
   B. $\frac{6}{8}$
   C. $\frac{9}{12}$
   D. *all of the above*

Revision 14

Hilde cut a pie into 4 equal pieces and ate one of the pieces. How much of the pie is still left?

   A. $\frac{1}{4}$
   B. $\frac{6}{7}$
   C. $\frac{6}{8}$
   D. $\frac{4}{12}$

Imagine the fifth-grade student who is weak at doing fractions. Perhaps the student knows $\frac{3}{4}$ is correct but struggles with conversions. The student assumes that there is one correct answer to a math problem, selects $\frac{3}{4}$ because that one is correct, and moves on to the next problem. Then again, maybe the teacher only uses "all of the above" when it's the correct answer. If students have caught on to this, they would select that alternative, and the teacher would not know if the students recognize these fractions as equivalent. Revision 14 allows the teacher to test the concept of fractions and conversion between equivalent fractions without the added confusion of the "all of the above" distractor.

Using "none of these" or "all of the above" makes the question more challenging. Rather than knowing that only one choice from the alternatives is correct, students must carefully analyze each alternative because they could all be correct or incorrect. This test-taking skill is very difficult for many students, especially younger ones. Teachers who like this format should use it sparingly and not always as the correct choice.

Guideline 15: List alternatives either vertically or horizontally.

Example 15

Use the table to answer the question.

Company	1997 Sales (in millions of dollars)	1998 Sales (in millions of dollars)
Allat	6.3	6.8
Edwas	5.7	6.5
Jemik	7.3	6.9
Zaller	9.2	9.1

Which company experienced the largest increase in sales from 1997 to 1998?

A. *Jemik*   C. *Allat*
B. *Edwas*   D. *Zaller*

Revision 15

Use the table to answer the question.

Company	1997 Sales (in millions of dollars)	1998 Sales (in millions of dollars)
Allat	6.3	6.8
Edwas	5.7	6.5
Jemik	7.3	6.9
Zaller	9.2	9.1

Which company experienced the largest increase in sales from 1997 to 1998?

    A. Allat   C. Jemik

    B. Edwas   D. Zaller

Test makers often list alternatives vertically and horizontally, as shown in Example 15, to save space and paper (see also Figure 5–3), but this format is confusing to some students. This is especially true when the correct answer is B or C. On some assessments, B is written to the right of A and C is written below A. On other tests, B is below A and C is to the right of A. To avoid potential confusion that may lead a student who knows the correct answer to marking a wrong choice, it is best to list all distractors in a single vertical list or across horizontally, a format which is limited to very short responses. Note that the alternatives were reordered in Revision 15 and put into alphabetical order to match the order in the table.

Guideline 16: Verify that each item has one and only one correct answer.

Example 16

The Union of Soviet Socialist Republics (USSR) is located in

    A. Europe and Asia

    B. North and South America

    C. Africa

    D. Australia

Revision 16

The country known as the Union of Soviet Socialist Republics (USSR), which no longer exists, was located in

    A. Europe and Asia

    B. North and South America

    C. Africa

    D. Australia

It should go without saying that every multiple-choice item should have one, and only one, correct answer. A few years ago, Example 16 was a good knowledge-level test item. Today, the USSR no longer exists as a single country, so, technically, there is no correct answer to the item as written in Example 16. Revision 16 refers to the country in its historical context, so there is a correct answer for that item.

For most test items, it is usually relatively simple for the teacher to identify an intended correct answer. It is ensuring that all the other distractors are incorrect and plausible at the same time that causes the greatest problems. Plausible distractors are those alternatives that students who really do not know the content or have the skills being tested are likely to choose. These distractors are clearly wrong to the knowledgeable and skilled student.

Sometimes teachers choose distractors because they are only partially correct or they are not the complete answer (see Example 11B). We do not endorse or recommend such practice. A distractor should be a wrong answer. Though the directions to multiple-choice items usually indicate that the student should choose the *best* answer, this is not an excuse for having distractors that could also be correct.

TRUE-FALSE ITEMS

Purpose and power

True-false items can be used effectively to test a student's factual knowledge. A relatively large number of these items can be administered in a relatively short period of time, allowing for broad content coverage. Scoring is objective and can be done quickly.

Testing higher levels of learning is difficult with true-false items, however. Few concepts can be phrased in terms that are absolutely true or absolutely false. As a result, in a true-false format, the teacher would have to include qualifications and exceptions in the statement, making the true-false item complicated and less effective as an assessment strategy.

Another limitation of the true-false format is that students have a 50 percent probability of answering correctly. Guessing can be limited by using modified true-false items, for which the student must correct a false statement to make it true. Of course, this strategy only works with false items, and guessing for true items is not detected.

Effective true-false items

As with multiple-choice items, there are several guidelines to follow when writing effective true-false items. These guidelines are detailed in the following list and are discussed in the following sections. Some guidelines that applied to the development of multiple-choice items also apply to true-false items.

Guidelines for Writing Effective True-False Test Items
1. Write items in clear and simple language, keeping vocabulary as simple as possible.
2. Base each item on a single central idea that is stated clearly and completely in the statement.
3. Avoid negative wording in the statement.
4. Avoid window dressing in the statement.
5. Avoid patterns when using qualifiers or absolute terms.
6. Use absolutely true or absolutely false statements for true-false items.
7. Include the source with a statement of opinion.
8. Indicate which word or phrase the student is to correct in a modified true-false item.

Guideline 1: Write items in clear and simple language, keeping vocabulary as simple as possible.

Example 1

In the fictional novel *Old Yeller*, a boy, in the absence of his father, assumes adult responsibilities by managing the family homestead, caring for his sibling, and dealing with tragedy, all the while be-friending a mangy mutt who saves his life several times while he is trying to be an adult.

_____ True   _____ False

Revision 1

Old Yeller is a story about how a boy learns that he is able to take on some of the responsibilities of an adult.

_____ True   _____ False

For students who have never read *Old Yeller*, this example tells the whole story. The intent when writing a true-false item is to ensure that students understand the statement and can determine whether it is true or false. Long, complicated statements with challenging vocabulary raise the reading load, as well as the anxiety level, for the student as she tries to decipher what the statement says and if all or any part of it is false. The revision has a single statement with relatively simple vocabulary that will be much clearer to the student. Note that the revision requires students to synthesize information from the story, which represents a higher-order cognitive level on Bloom's Taxonomy.

Guideline 2: Base each item on a single central idea that is stated clearly and completely in the statement.

Example 2

All quadrilaterals are polygons, and all triangles are quadrilaterals.

_____ True   _____ False

Revision 2

All quadrilaterals are polygons.

_____ True   _____ False

All triangles are quadrilaterals.

_____ True   _____ False

In Example 2, the first statement is true, but the second statement is false. The use of multiple statements within the same item not only confuses the student and complicates the problem but may also lead to inappropriate conclusions about content knowledge. Students may answer the item correctly because they only know one of the several ideas included in the item is false. Similarly, Example 1 shows a statement with several parts, each of which must be analyzed separately to determine whether it is true or false. In a single true-false item, avoid multiple statements that are partly true and partly false. If the item were separated into single-issue items (see Revision 2), the teacher would have a better understanding of what the student knows and does not know.

Guideline 3: Avoid negative wording in the statement.

Example 3

Mark Twain is *not* the author of *Moby Dick*.

_____ True   _____ False

Revision 3

Mark Twain wrote *Moby Dick*.

_____ True   _____ False

The statement in Example 3 is true because Mark Twain is not the author of Moby Dick. However, think about a student having to answer this question during a stressful testing situation. The student knows Herman Melville is the author of Moby Dick. So the student reasons, "Mark Twain is not and that information is incorrect, and therefore the answer is false, I mean true, no I mean, I mean. . . ." False statements have a negative connotation. People expect incorrect information to be false. When a negative is used in the true-false statement, the student is really trying to sort out two negative ideas.

Guideline 4: Avoid window dressing in the statement.

Example 4

Milk fat does not naturally mix with the rest of milk and it usually floats to the top of the milk container. Rather than having to shake the milk or skim off the milk fat, a process is used to break up the milk fat so that it mixes well throughout the rest of the milk. This process is called homogenization.

_____ True   _____ False

Revision 4

The process of breaking up milk fat and mixing it throughout the milk is called homogenization.

_____ True   _____ False

It is exhausting just reading Example 4. There are so many extra words, when the real question can be succinctly written in a single sentence, as shown in Revision 4. When a true-false item is as long as this example, students begin to wonder which if any word is wrong and may choose false because they get lost in all the details. They may view an item like this example as a trick question. If your goal is to determine if students know the definition of homogenization, then simply ask for the definition. If the goal is to find out if they can explain the process of homogenization and the reason that it is done, then the item would be better written as a constructed-response item, as discussed in Chapter 3.

Guideline 5: Avoid patterns when using qualifiers or absolute terms.

Example 5

Tornadoes *always occur in the summer.*

_____ True   _____ False

Revision 5

Tornadoes may occur at any time of the year.

_____ True   _____ False

Students have learned to clue in on absolute terms such as *always* and *never*. When these terms appear in true-false items, students are likely to choose "false." Similarly, qualifiers such as *sometimes* and *usually* indicate to students that the answer is probably "true." There are two ways to deal with this problem. The first is to avoid using absolute terms and qualifiers. The second is to be sure to select some true-false items that are true when they contain the term *always* or *never*. Similarly, use some true-false items that are false when qualifiers are included. When you avoid an obvious pattern, students learn to not use these terms as extraneous clues to the correct answer. Here is an example of the use of a qualifier when the statement is false followed by an example of the use of an absolute term when the statement is true:

During the summer, the sun is usually directly overhead at noon in South Carolina.

_____ True   _____ False

A neutral atom always contains the same number of protons and electrons.

_____ True   _____ False

Guideline 6: Use absolutely true or absolutely false statements for true-false items.

Example 6
The sun rises in the east each morning.

_____ True   _____ False

Revision 6
To see a sunrise, a person would look toward the east in the morning.

_____ True   _____ False

or

On the first day of spring, the sun rises due east.

_____ True   _____ False

There is no ambiguity for the student when a statement is absolutely true or absolutely false. With some items like Example 6, students who know more are likely to be confused by the statement and spend time trying to guess what the teacher is looking for rather than basing their answer on what they know. Generally speaking, sunrise is in the east. However, it isn't due east every day. Actually, the sun rises due east only on the first day of spring and the first day of autumn. Students who know that sunrise varies from south of east to north of east and back again over the course of a year will have a hard time with what seems to be a very easy question.

The first item in Revision 6 is a bit more general and shouldn't pose a problem for most students. The second item in Revision 6 is more specific and could only be used if the students have had an opportunity to study the pattern of sunrise. Another way to deal with Example 6 is to make it a modified true-false item, so students who mark it "false" can explain their reasoning. Teachers will then know if students simply lack general knowledge about sunrise or compass directions or if they have read more into the item.

Guideline 7: Include the source with a statement of opinion.

For the following items, refer to the story *Bowled Over* presented in Guideline 5 (page 87).

Example 7

Bowling parties are fun.

_____ True   _____ False

Revision 7

Jackie thought that having a bowling party would be fun.

_____ True   _____ False

Example 7 is an opinion and, therefore, is not necessarily true unless attributed to the author. This item requires a very simple revision: include the author's name in the statement, as shown in Revision 7.

Guideline 8: Indicate which word or phrase the student is to correct in a modified true-false item.

Example 8

If the statement is false, make a correction so that the statement will be true.

Scientists believe the earliest dinosaurs appeared during the *Triassic* ~~Permian~~ Period.

_____ True   __√__ False

Scientists believe the earliest dinosaurs appeared during the *Mesozoic Era* ~~Permian Period.~~

_____ True   __√__ False

Scientists believe the earliest dinosaurs ~~appeared~~ *became extinct* during the *Cretaceous* ~~Permian~~ Period.

_____ True   __√__ False

Revision 8

If the statement is false, make a correction to the underlined term so that the statement will be true.

Scientists believe the earliest dinosaurs appeared during the <u>Permian</u> Period.

_____ True   __√__ False

Students could make several different changes to Example 8 to correct the statement. They could replace the term *Permian* with the correct term *Triassic*. Or they could replace the phrase *Permian Period* with *Mesozoic Era*, which is also correct. Or they could make two changes and modify the statement to say, "Scientists believe that the dinosaurs *became extinct* during the *Cretaceous* Period (or Mesozoic Era)." In other words, lots of possible modifications would result in a correct statement, so the teacher may not know if students have the specific information that she was testing. To simplify scoring and avoid a situation in which almost anything is correct, a teacher might highlight the word or phrase the student should change if the item is false, by underlining or italicizing it. Notice the underlining in Revision 8 directs the student to change Permian if the statement is false. When students are not directed to the expected change, anything goes and the student who lacks the knowledge being tested is free to make correct, but simplified, revisions to the item.

MATCHING ITEMS

Purpose and power of effective matching items

Like true-false and multiple-choice items, matching items allow the teacher to assess a lot of content knowledge in a relatively short period of time. Matching items assess primarily recall of factual information and associations among those facts. They are relatively easy to construct and scoring is objective and quick.

Matching items have two parts: (1) a list of item stems, called premises, on the left and (2) a list of responses on the right. This assessment form can be thought of as a series of multiple-choice items. Each premise is a stem that has all the responses listed in the right column as possible choices. An example may help to clarify the structure of this type of item. Imagine a test of Spanish vocabulary. In the column on the left, a list of English nouns would be the premises, and, in the column on the right, the Spanish terms would be the responses. Matching items are more efficient at assessing knowledge than multiple-choice items because they can avoid duplication by combining several stems with a long list of distractors.

Effective matching items

Many of the guidelines that govern the development of multiple-choice items also apply to matching items. In the following sections, we discuss several of those guidelines with specific matching applications and a few unique rules.

Guidelines for Writing Effective Matching Test Items
1. Begin each set of matching items with a clear set of directions.
2. Choose premises that are alike and responses that are alike.

3. Use responses that are plausible to students who lack the knowledge and/or skills tested by the item.
4. Make the number of responses greater than or less than the number of premises.
5. Avoid extremely long lists of premises and responses.
6. Arrange premises and responses in logical order, if one exists.

Guideline 1: Begin each set of matching items with a clear set of directions.

Example 1

Match Column A to Column B.

Revision 1

Different historic events are listed in Column A. On the line to the left of each event, write the letter of the date from Column B that tells when the event occurred. Dates may be used more than once.

Clear directions tell the student what to do. Revision 1 is specific in terms of what is being matched and how students are to record their answers. Directions should tell whether responses can be used once, more than once, or not at all.

Guideline 2: Choose premises that are alike and responses that are alike.

Example 2

Match the names in Column A with the terms in Column B. Place the letter of the term in Column B on the line preceding the name in Column A.

Column A	Column B
_____ *Bridge to Terabithia*	A. *name of a novel*
_____ *Katherine Paterson*	B. *Jessie's school*
_____ *Lark Creek Elementary*	C. *author of a book*
_____ *Jessie Aarons*	D. *character in a book*

Revision 2

Match each character listed in Column A with the name of the book in Column B. Place the letter for the name of the book on the line preceding the name of the character who appeared in the book. Books may be used more than once.

Column A	Column B
_____ Aunt Willie	a. *Bridge to Terabithia*
_____ Brian Robeson	b. *Hatchet*
_____ Cassie Logan	c. *Roll of Thunder, Hear My Cry*
_____ Mr. Granger	d. *The Summer of the Swans*
_____ Sarah Godfrey	

When premises and/or responses include a variety of categories, as in Example 2, the item becomes more confusing. Teachers also find it difficult to give clear information in the directions about what is to be matched. When categories in a column are not consistent, guessing becomes easier because some responses may not seem plausible to a student who lacks knowledge. Students can play the elimination game, thinking, "I may not be sure about this Katherine Paterson part, but I know that Lake Creek Elementary is a school and since the response is 'Jessie's school,' Jessie is probably the character in the book." At this point, the student now has a good chance of getting the Katherine Paterson part correct simply by guessing.

With a little more reasoning that an author probably isn't named *Bridge to Terabithia*, the student has now correctly matched all the premises with all the responses without having ever read the book. Similarly, when premises or responses are not grammatically consistent with one another, students may find clues in the list for premises or responses so the teacher will not know if the student actually knows the information or was merely successful at using clues and guessing at the answers.

In the revision, Column A is a list of characters and Column B is a list of titles. Note that we used lowercase letters before the names of the books in the revision. We chose lowercase letters to make it easier to distinguish the letter for the response from the capital letter that begins the title. Uppercase letters, numbers, or Roman numerals are also acceptable ways to label matching items.

Some teachers have students draw lines between the premises and responses. This is an acceptable technique for students in the lower grades who are still struggling with handwriting. Drawing lines for matching can get very confusing for the student and the teacher grading the papers when more than three or four items are to be matched or when premises or responses are used more than once.

Guideline 3: Use responses that are plausible to students who lack the knowledge and/or skills tested by the item.

Example 3

Column A contains a list of names of bones in the human body. Column B names parts of the body. On each line in Column A, write the letter of the body part telling where the bone is found. Each response in Column B may be used more than once or not at all.

Column A	Column B
_____ femur	A. arm
_____ fibula	B. *brain*
_____ humerus	C. chest
_____ radius	D. head
_____ rib	E. *heart*
_____ sternum	F. leg
_____ tibia	G. *stomach*
_____ ulna	

Revision 3

Column A contains a list of names of bones in the human body. Column B names parts of the body. On each line in Column A, write the letter of the body part telling where the bone is found. Each response in Column B may be used more than once or not at all.

Column A	Column B
_____ femur	A. arm
_____ fibula	B. chest
_____ humerus	C. foot
_____ radius	D. hand
_____ rib	E. head
_____ sternum	F. leg
_____ tibia	
_____ ulna	

In Example 3, it is unlikely students will choose responses B (brain), E (heart), or G (stomach) because these are organs *protected* by bones and, in discussions of body parts, they do not hold the same meaning for a student as arm, leg, head, and chest, parts of the body that are visible to them. As a result, these responses are probably not plausible to students. Just as it is difficult to find plausible distractors when writing multiple-choice items, it is challenging to write column entries in a matching item because each option in the second column must be a possible match for each premise in the first column.

Note that in Revision 3, two of the responses are used three times each and one of the responses is used twice. Students who are not experienced with matching items in which a response can be used more than twice may find this situation unsettling; less confident students may be tempted to change their answers. The idea is to not be predictable or follow patterns that students can use as clues to guessing the correct answer. Remember, a teacher wants to find out what students have learned, not how clever they are at figuring out answers because of clues in the test items.

Guideline 4: Make the number of responses greater than or less than the number of premises.

Example 4

Match the country on the left with the continent where it is located on the right. Write the letter of the continent on the line preceding the country.

Country	Continent
_____ Algeria	a. Africa
_____ Belgium	b. Asia
_____ China	c. Europe
_____ Peru	d. North America
_____ United States	e. South America

Revision 4

Match the country on the left with the continent where it is located on the right. Write the letter of the continent on the line preceding the country. Continents may be used more than once.

Country	Continent
_____ Algeria	a. Africa
_____ Argentina	b. Asia
_____ Belgium	c. Europe
_____ Brazil	d. North America
_____ China	e. South America
_____ Italy	
_____ Peru	
_____ United States	
_____ Zaire	

When there is the same number of premises and responses, students can eliminate possibilities. This increases the likelihood of their responding correctly when they do not actually know all the information. Another way to deal with this problem is to allow responses to be used more than once. Note that in Revision 4, one of the responses is used three times while two of the responses are each used twice.

Also note that the column headings are "Country" and "Continent" rather than "Column A" and "Column B." Students may find this format easier because they don't have to remember that Column A has the countries and Column B has the continents. Other students may find it more difficult to sort out the left column from the right. Teachers should use their best judgment and choose the format that works best for them and their students.

Guideline 5: Avoid extremely long lists of premises and responses.

Example 5

Match the event listed on the left with the year in which it occurred on the right. Write the year on the line preceding the event. Years may be used more than once.

Event	Year
_____ Astronauts landed on moon	1776
_____ *Civil War started*	1789
_____ Constitution of U.S. was ratified	*1861*
_____ Hawaii became a state of the U.S.	1920
_____ Johnson signed Civil Rights Act	1941
_____ President Kennedy was assassinated	1950
_____ Revolutionary War fought	1963
_____ Declaration Independence signed	1964

_____ T. Marshall joined Supreme Court	*1967*
_____ *Truman was president*	*1969*
_____ U.S. declared war on Japan	
_____ Washington became president	
_____ Women got the right to vote	
_____ *And so on . . .*	

Revision 5

Match the event listed on the left with the year in which it occurred on the right. Write the year on the line preceding the event. Years may be used more than once.

Event	**Year**
_____ Astronauts landed on moon	1920
_____ Johnson signed Civil Rights Act	1941
_____ Hawaii became a state of the U.S.	1950
_____ President Kennedy was assassinated	1963
_____ U.S. declared war on Japan	1964
_____ Women got the right to vote	1969

Frankly, we got tired of listing all the premises and all the responses for Example 5. Imagine how the students feel when faced with a seemingly endless list. Sometimes the list runs onto the next page and creates even more extraneous hardships for the students. Long lists of premises and responses simply confuse the reader and result in students taking much longer to answer the item. Using several matching items with not more than five to ten premises and responses will enable the teacher to assess all the information she wants without making the item unnecessarily complicated.

Guideline 6: Arrange premises and responses in logical order, if one exists.

Example 6

Match the shape listed in Column A with the number of sides listed in Column B. Place the letter of the number of sides on the line preceding the shape. The number of sides may be used more than once or may not be used at all.

Column A	**Column B**
_____ *triangle*	A. *10 sides*
_____ *square*	B. *4 sides*
_____ *rectangle*	C. *3 sides*
_____ *quadrilateral*	D. *5 sides*
_____ *rhombus*	E. *8 sides*
_____ *pentagon*	
_____ *octagon*	

Match the shape listed in Column A with the number of sides listed in Column B. Place the letter for the number of sides on the line preceding the shape. The number of sides may be used more than once or may not be used at all.

Column A	Column B
_____ octagon	A. 3 sides
_____ pentagon	B. 4 sides
_____ quadrilateral	C. 5 sides
_____ rectangle	D. 8 sides
_____ rhombus	E. 10 sides
_____ square	
_____ triangle	

The shapes and number of sides in Example 6 were listed rather haphazardly. When students proceed through the matching task, they will have to search both columns because there is no pattern to how the terms and numbers are listed. The order provided in Revision 6 makes it easier to find both the shape (alphabetical order) and the number of sides (numerical order). Revisions 2, 3, 4, and 5 also show premises and responses listed in alphabetical order. The years in Example 5 are listed in numerical order. Providing a logical order makes the item more organized and easier to follow and sort through. Students avoid wasting time rereading all premises and responses as they search for the correct answer. Remember, the purpose of the test is to determine what students know, not if they can sort through a long jumbled list.

DATA ANALYSIS

One of the benefits of using selected-response items is the ease of data analysis. Scoring is a simple matter of determining if students chose the correct answers. An answer is either right or wrong; there is no partial credit. To determine how many students answered a question correctly, the teacher simply has to count up the number of student papers with the correct answer selected.

For multiple-choice items, it is interesting to look at how frequently students chose the various alternatives for each question. This technique, referred to as a frequency analysis, can provide valuable information to the teacher about misconceptions and common errors that students make when they have not mastered the concepts tested. The frequency analysis will also illustrate weak distractors because few, if any, students will select them. The teacher can use this information to revise the test item before using it again.

A frequency analysis is done by counting up the number of students who selected each alternative for a particular item. A frequency analysis for the science item in Figure 5–1 is shown in Figure 5–4. Notice that fewer than half the students chose the correct answer, 1, which means that more than half the students do not understand the concept being tested. Because a large percentage of students chose each of the two wrong answers, it appears that many students may just be guessing. The teacher can use this information as an indication that further instruction is needed. Had the teacher not analyzed the data, he would never have known that students had not learned the content and would most likely have continued with new lessons, never addressing the learning problem in his classes.

A teacher can do a similar analysis with responses to true-false items. Simply determine how many students answered "true" to each item and how many answered "false." If a teacher determines that most of the class chose "true" for a false statement, the teacher knows that content needs to be revisited. For modified true-false items, the teacher should also determine how many students who answered "false" were able to correct the false statement accurately. By reviewing the incorrect changes students made, teachers will gain some insight about content students are having difficulty with, as well as misconceptions they may have.

The same idea works for matching items. In this case, the teacher wants to determine if the students are having trouble with a few premises and/or responses or if the entire set is a problem. Information from a class of students for matching Revision 4, the item about the location of countries on continents, is reported in Figure 5–5.

By reviewing the answer choices made by the students, the teacher can see that most students know where most of the countries in this list are located. For example, twenty students knew that Argentina is in South America, eighteen knew that Belgium is in Europe, and twenty-three knew that the United States is in North America. The frequency analysis does show that some students had trouble with each country, and the teacher should review those papers to see if the same few students are making the errors. If that is the case, then the teacher needs to provide targeted assistance to those students who had difficulty. The analysis also reveals that most students do not know where Algeria and Zaire are located. The information

	Answer Choices			
	1	2	3	No Answer
Number of Students	60	44	33	3
Percent of Students	42.9	31.4	23.6	2.1

FIGURE 5–4   *Frequency analysis for the science item*

	Africa	Asia	Europe	North America	South America
Algeria	3	7	5	3	7
Argentina	2	2	0	1	20
Belgium	1	1	18	2	3
Brazil	2	3	1	1	18
China	0	18	1	1	5
Italy	1	1	22	1	0
Peru	0	3	2	1	19
United States	0	1	1	23	0
Zaire	0	9	6	0	10

FIGURE 5–5   *Analysis of student responses to social studies matching item*

indicates that additional instruction is needed for the whole class about the location of these countries.

ISSUES

As with all test questions, issues of reliability, validity, and fairness must be addressed when writing selected-response items. To be valid, the item must assess what it is intended to assess. A reliable item will be answered by students with similar knowledge the same way each time. By following the guidelines for writing good selected-response items, teachers have a greater chance of ensuring the validity and reliability of the test items they write. The guidelines will also help teachers write items that are fair for all students, but there are special problems associated with selected-response items that are important.

Selected-response items seem easy to some because, after all, the answer is on the test paper. For some students, choosing the correct answer from a set of alternatives may require some degree of guessing. Guessing is not a skill that comes easily to all students. As an example, consider the situation in which students are given a fifty-item multiple-choice test on which each item has four alternatives. Two students proceed through the test and answer thirty-eight items with confidence. For the remaining twelve items, one student eliminates some choices and makes educated guesses. Chances are, he has chosen correctly three times for these twelve guesses (25 percent of the time). The other student, not comfortable with this test-taking strategy, leaves the twelve answers blank since he is not sure of the answers.

How can teachers deal with this difference? We recommend that teachers teach appropriate test-taking strategies, such as encouraging students to eliminate alternatives they are sure are incorrect and to make educated guesses among the remaining alternatives. However, teachers should not encourage students to make random guesses. Also, when using selected-response tests in the classroom, it is important to provide ample time for students to complete a test.

Another issue to consider is the reading load of the item. Teachers often hear a student say, "I read it wrong." Math, science, and social studies items are often more challenging than they should be because of the level of reading required to interpret the test item. Teachers should write items in simple language that conveys the correct meaning. Also, students should be taught to dissect test items by looking for key words or words that could be overlooked and might lead to the wrong answer. For example, if a math problem asks for a series of numbers in ascending order, students should know to cue in on terms like *increasing*. Otherwise, they may select the alternative that has the correct numbers for the series, but in decreasing order.

Selected-response items allow the teacher to assess a lot of knowledge in a relatively short period of time and to score those items quickly. However, except for testing situations, these types of items do not relate directly to real-world problem solving. Rarely will anyone encounter a problem situation with two to four alternatives spelled out in front of them. Most real-world problems are more complex and do not lend themselves to picking from a few clear-cut choices. The point is that the connection between selected-response test items and the real world is tenuous at best. While they serve as useful assessment strategies in the classroom, overreliance on them is a disservice to students.

The selected-response approach to assessment has the strength of facilitating broad content coverage. The guidelines in this chapter emphasize the challenge of writing selected-response items. This skill may seem overwhelming at first, but with attention to the details mentioned herein, the results from selected-response tests will be an important part of the picture of student learning that a teacher must create to guide instructional planning and to give students grades. If he uses this approach in combination with other approaches described in this book, a teacher is able to gain an accurate portrayal of what a student knows and is able to do.

6 | ASSESSMENT PORTFOLIOS

For some fields and professions, portfolios have a longstanding tradition as a tool to demonstrate abilities and accomplishments. Artists, architects, and performers might bring a portfolio showing past work when interviewing for a position or contract. The use of portfolios for assessment of student learning was initiated to follow this tradition.

A common definition of an assessment portfolio is "a collection of student work that tells the story of learning" (Kuhs 1997). This collection of work must be purposeful in that it reveals a student's progress or achievement in a focused area. A portfolio is not just a collection of individual tasks; it is an integrated whole. The pieces of work that are included should be related to different dimensions of performance that are the focus of the portfolio assessment. From classroom to classroom and situation to situation, the purpose of the collections will vary. However, there are two common portfolio types: showcase and growth.

A showcase portfolio includes only a student's best work. A student portfolio that contains the best essays, reports, and poems would showcase the student's writing in different genres. A mathematics portfolio might showcase the use of problem-solving approaches such as using a table, a computer, diagrams, or trial and error. A showcase portfolio in any subject area would include pieces of work that demonstrate best accomplishments related to defined dimensions of student performance in that subject.

A portfolio that portrays the development of student knowledge over time is a growth portfolio. The samples of work in a growth portfolio are from different times of the year and document what students can do at the time they finish the portfolio that they could not do earlier with regard to specific learning outcomes. When the goal is to demonstrate growth, early pieces of work showing errors or exhibiting misunderstandings might be included with later pieces of work demonstrating improvement related to the initial areas of difficulty. Some teachers encourage students to make corrections or edit early papers to show the acquisition of skills at a later time.

In the introduction of a science unit, for example, a teacher might ask students to write an explanation of their understandings of an important concept such as why it rains. The students' writings may reveal misconceptions of key scientific phenomena that will be studied. After investigating the appropriate concepts involved in the rain cycle, students might be asked to write an explanation based on what they have learned. The differences between the first and second pieces of writing would clearly demonstrate the development of their understandings of the key science concepts that were taught. A collection of such paired writings, or a series of pieces with a common focus collected over time, evolves into a growth portfolio that documents the development of student knowledge.

PORTFOLIO ELEMENTS

Certain elements characterize portfolios, regardless of the type of portfolio being assembled. Of course, portfolios include actual pieces of student work such as student journal entries, long-term projects, homework, class assignments, tests, essays, worksheets, and drawings. Other portfolio entries are items that provide documentation of student performance such as photographs of projects or presentations, audiotapes of student reading, videotapes of performances or oral presentations, computer printouts, and photocopies of student work. All such items are commonly referred to as artifacts. Sometimes technology can be used to maintain a portfolio electronically if scanners are available; then the portfolio becomes an electronic image that documents student work.

It is always a good idea to put a date on each artifact in the collection. This is especially important if the portfolio is intended to show growth over time. But even in a showcase portfolio, the dates will provide insights. For example, in a mathematics showcase portfolio, a piece that was included to document the ability to organize information in a table might show weaknesses in the ability to solve problems. Another piece that showcases problem solving might seem contradictory if the pieces did not have dates on them. Perhaps the paper on using tables was done early in the year while the problem-solving paper was done much later and no contradiction in accomplishment exists. Yet without dates, the sequence is unknown.

Other elements of the portfolio serve to organize the collection and articulate the story of learning. A table of contents like that in Figure 6–1 commonly introduces the collection. In some cases the table is annotated, providing information about student learning. For example, when Jamie Johnson wrote statements in his table of contents, the teacher was able to see that he was aware of different problem-solving strategies. When annotations give the rationale for selecting the piece, the student's interpretation of how the piece is connected to the evaluative criteria is apparent. In this manner the table of contents provides an organizational framework that also tells the story of learning.

In other cases a portfolio log like the one in Figure 6–2 takes the place of the table of contents. The teacher, sometimes in cooperation with

Problem-Solving Portfolio of Jamie Johnson	Grade Two
Table of Contents	**Entry Number**
Pattern Block Activity This paper shows how I can use trial and error. I had to try over and over to find the pieces that cover the shape if I could only use 8.	1
Farm Animal Problem I made a drawing to figure out how many legs 8 chickens, 3 pigs, and 5 cows would have. I also had to count.	2
Test Paper This paper shows how I can add and subtract to solve story problems.	3

FIGURE 6–1   *Table of contents for problem-solving portfolio*

students, designs the log as an outline of the areas of learning that they are going to document in the portfolio. In finishing the portfolio log, a student would identify which pieces of work in the collection match particular areas of learning. One of the advantages of using a portfolio log is that, in a glance, the teacher and student can see areas of learning that are being addressed and those that are not. The example in Figure 6–2 shows the areas of writing in which Elena has demonstrated learning during the first half of the school year. The student has included artifacts related to organization, sentence formation, and conventions, but there is no entry in the column labeled "Style" because she is still working on developing style. It is not necessary to have an entry in every box in the grid during the year. However, a completed portfolio should have at least one entry in each column to document the student's accomplishment in each area.

Sometimes a portfolio will include a letter to the reviewer or some other introductory statement. Such introductions should be based on the student's reflections about his work and are especially important when the portfolio is to be examined by someone outside the classroom. Thus, if parents, a principal, or next year's teacher will be examining the collection, the letter might provide an explanation of what the portfolio means to the student. Sometimes this introduction is an integrative statement that brings to-

			Sentence	
Writing Portfolio of Elena Paloma **Fourth Grade**				
Artifacts	**Organization**	**Style**	**Sentence Formation**	**Conventions**
Limerick	Sept. 29			Sept. 29
Personal letter			Oct. 15	Oct. 15
Fictional Story "Bessie"	Dec. 8		Dec. 8	Dec. 8
Poem "Surprise"				Dec. 15
Report	Jan. 11			

FIGURE 6–2 *Portfolio log for writing portfolio*

gether all of the pieces of work to describe student learning in terms of the purpose of the portfolio.

For example, if a teacher decided to use a portfolio approach to prepare students for the state's writing assessment, then the portfolio may include pieces to document growth in organization, style, sentence formation, and conventions. The letter or integrative statement would be the child's discussion of how the pieces of work show development of these writing elements. Here is an example of such a letter:

Dear Mom and Dad,

This year in fourth grade we have been learning about four elements of writing. They are organization, style, sentence formation, and conventions. The pieces in this portfolio show my best work in writing. The first piece is a story I wrote that has a clear beginning, middle, and end. The words I used in the limerick I wrote about classmates are descriptive words that paint a picture. I am getting better at forming sentences. The book report I wrote shows this. We also learned how to use quotation marks this year. I used them when my characters talked in my fictional story in the portfolio.

As students assemble portfolios, the teacher often asks them to identify goals for future learning as they examine their past work. Such statements about learning goals may be included in the letter to the reviewer. Students may even give ideas about how they plan to accomplish those goals in their statements. For example, the previous student letter might have ended with a statement such as, "I still need to work on putting more details in my stories. The teacher and I talked about making lists of descriptive words I might use before I do my revision."

Some teachers require students to write cover sheets containing reflective statements for each artifact in the collection. Such statements offer the student's rationale for including the piece or contain other reflections about the student's learning. Strategies to help students learn to reflect on their work and write different types of reflections will be offered later in the chapter.

Physically, portfolios take many shapes and forms. A portfolio created by a professional such as an artist, an architect, or a person in advertising is typically a collection of his or her work assembled in a large leather carrier. Simplicity characterizes portfolio use in classrooms. In some cases, student-decorated file folders are appropriate, while in others, the teacher may want to use boxes or another type of container. Many teachers use plastic crates and provide each student with a hanging folder in which to collect pieces of work.

PORTFOLIO PROCESS

The effective use of portfolios results in the change of the culture of the classroom (Spandel and Culham 1994). In such classrooms, students assume a greater role in the evaluation process by learning to review their own work as they select pieces that document their learning. Eventually a cycle develops in which students are encouraged to reflect on their work and sometimes revise it. They then set goals for future learning and work with the teacher to identify strategies to pursue those goals. This cycle of reflective activity can be referred to as the portfolio process. Within this process, students acquire the ability to assess what they know, what they need to learn, and what they can do to accomplish that learning. This portfolio process involves students in the five phases of activity outlined in the following list. Each of these phases will be described in the following sections.

Phases of the Portfolio Process

1. Students learn about the purpose of the portfolio and the criteria that will be the basis for assessment.
2. Students create working portfolios that are accumulations of artifacts related to the areas of learning and the evaluative criteria.
3. Students review their working portfolios periodically and select pieces to keep.
4. Students finalize their collections in preparation for review.

5. Students reflect on their accomplishments, organize their collections, and set goals for future learning. (Adapted from Spandel and Culham 1994)

Phase 1

The first phase of the portfolio process is to help students understand the purpose of the portfolio. To do this a teacher might, for example, tell students, "We want to create a portfolio to show your family your growth or improvement in using the elements of writing." In this manner the teacher establishes the purpose of the portfolio and tells students what types of work will go into the collection. As the teacher and students discuss the purpose, consideration should be given to the criteria that will be used to evaluate the final collection. Scoring guides such as those discussed in Chapter 4 can be developed for use in the evaluation of the portfolio. Ideally, students will participate in determining the criteria. When students participate in the development of the criteria and scoring guides, they begin to develop an understanding of expected standards of performance. The guides then become tools to help students decide what pieces of work they want to save for their collection. Examples of such scoring guides are offered later in this chapter.

Phase 2

In the next phase of the portfolio process, students begin to accumulate artifacts related to the areas of learning and the evaluative criteria. This collection is often called a working portfolio. Learning to select pieces is an acquired skill. If portfolio use is to be effective, teachers must help students develop the ability to examine and critique their own work. In order for students to participate in the portfolio process, they must learn to be critical and reflective at each stage of the process.

To help students develop these skills, teachers find it useful to ask students to write reflections about their work and include these in their working portfolios. This kind of reflection does not come naturally. Students must be taught to reflect on their work. Having students write statements about what they learned while doing the task also helps them develop the habit of thinking about their work in terms of evaluative criteria. After completing a piece of work, a student might write reflections on the back of the piece itself or on an attached sheet. The teacher might ask students to answer the following questions:

Why is this piece in my portfolio?
What did I learn while doing the task?
What do I want to remember about doing this paper?
What did I do especially well in this piece of work?
What do I need to work on?

Student responses will include statements such as: "This is about adding more than two numbers," or "I learned how to use the computer to make a circle graph when we did this project," or "I thought this was hard to do and had to get help." These notes are very helpful when a student is reviewing work or selecting pieces for the final assessment portfolio.

Phase 3

The third phase of the process involves periodic examination of the working portfolio. If students have too many pieces to examine, the task of selecting pieces that document targeted learning may become overwhelming. Therefore, it is important to control the accumulation of artifacts in the working portfolio. In primary grades, where children may do several pieces of work each day, teachers may ask students to examine their working portfolio each week. After selecting the pieces they want to keep in the working portfolio, students might take other pieces home to keep parents informed about class work. In higher grades, such reviews of the working portfolio could occur less often because older students are able to manage the complexity of sorting through work done over a longer period of time. Also, in the upper grades the type of work that students would keep for portfolios is likely to be complex and completed over a span of time, so they would accumulate fewer pieces.

Initially teachers might help students consider particular pieces of work for the collection that would be appropriate. In doing this, a teacher might be very directive, for example, telling students that an essay they just wrote should be put in their working portfolio. In other cases, after completing a piece of work, a teacher might plan to discuss if this student work should be saved in the working portfolio. To model the thought process involved in selecting pieces, the teacher might ask:

> What did we learn in doing this task?
> Do you remember what we said about our portfolio? What did we say was its purpose?
> Can anyone tell me why someone would, or why someone would not, want to put this piece of work in our collection?
> What will this piece show we have learned?

Another way to help students would involve conferencing or asking informal questions so students can talk about why they did or did not select a piece for the collection. In this context it is important for the teacher to help students understand when pieces other than those a student selected provide more appropriate documentation of the targeted areas of learning.

As was suggested in the discussion of rubrics in Chapter 4, encouraging peer support in reviewing student work helps students develop an understanding of the evaluative criteria. Peer support during the portfolio process also has many benefits. It would require a great deal of time for a teacher to have a separate conversation with every student about the selection of each piece of work. As students learn to evaluate their work, many of the decisions about the collection become routine. Yet, it is helpful for students to have someone to consult during the process of selecting pieces. Many times students can answer one another's questions about format or about whether a particular paper fits a certain area of learning covered by the portfolio. Without such peer assistance, the process of putting the final portfolio together could become very frustrating. Working with peers and not having to check every detail with the teacher helps students develop confidence. It also makes the process more efficient and manageable for the teacher, who is there to provide guidance when it is needed.

Phase 4

In phase 4 of the process, students finalize the selection of pieces in preparation for review. Such a review may occur periodically during the year, perhaps at the end of each report period, or at the end of the year. In some instances students will edit work as they reflect on it. For example, a student might revise a piece of writing and include both the revised and the original papers in the portfolio. In mathematics a student might demonstrate increased understanding of a procedure by correcting all errors on a paper she did previously. In both cases, the students would discuss their newly acquired learning in their written reflections and comment on how they applied this new understanding to old papers.

As part of the process of finalizing the collection, teachers usually ask students to provide rationales or explanations for why they selected particular pieces. Different students might choose different pieces of work for their final collections. As students draft rationale statements, they may examine the reflections they made on the pieces of work in their working portfolio. When the portfolio is going to be made public, or graded, or passed on to next year's teacher, it is important that students make the basis of their choices explicit.

Phase 5

The final phase of the process involves the student in organizing the collection and writing statements to tell the story of his learning for a particular audience. As we mentioned earlier, the form such statements take may vary. A letter to the reviewer, integrative statements, an annotated table of contents, or separate reflective statements on each piece might be used separately or in combination to organize and finalize the collection.

Decisions about this feature of the portfolio are influenced by the eventual use of the portfolio. If only the teacher and students in the class will be reviewing the document, less detail might be needed and a simple table of contents or portfolio log would be appropriate. If, on the other hand, the portfolio is to be examined by the parents, more elaborate approaches such as reflections on each piece, letters to the parents, or an annotated table of contents might be appropriate. In lower grade levels students might even rehearse conversations about the work in their portfolios in preparation for a school-family conference that centers around the student presenting the portfolio to family members.

Regardless of the form students use in finalizing the collection, the student must communicate the connection of the pieces to the evaluative criteria. Often this process provides the context for setting goals for future learning, especially if the portfolio review occurs at the end of each grading period. Asking students to identify personal goals for learning is a natural next step in the portfolio process. This can be done as part of a conversation with the teacher. Students could put the goals in writing as a part of the completed portfolio itself or they could communicate them during a school-family conference.

The reflection and goal-setting part of the portfolio process is sometimes the most important part. Again, this will be difficult for students at first and they are apt to focus their goals on areas of learning where they will readily see their progress, such as spelling and punctuation. At first the teacher may prompt the students to include goals that may be hard for them to state. For example, they might need to work on the organization of thoughts in their writing or improve their writing style through the selective use of descriptive words. The main purpose of this goal-setting activity is to help students focus on what they need to know. Also, helping them identify strategies to accomplish their goals gives students a plan to follow to reach their goals.

STEPS IN PLANNING PORTFOLIO ASSESSMENT

Planning is an important element of successful portfolio assessment. We offer the following steps to guide teachers in planning effective use of portfolio assessment.

Step 1. Decide what areas of learning are to be the focus of the portfolio.

To do this, a teacher should begin by examining curriculum guides and materials and asking, "What areas of student learning could be assessed using a portfolio approach?" The following lists suggest areas of student learning that teachers might choose as a focus for student portfolios.

A Mathematics Portfolio

Collects and uses data to support conclusions.
Recognizes, extends, and creates patterns.
Uses various strategies to solve problems.
Makes generalizations and creates classification systems.

A Language Arts Portfolio

Comprehends and interprets literature.
Uses the elements of good writing (organization, style, sentence formation, and conventions).
Uses oral language to provide information or express ideas.

An Interdisciplinary Portfolio
Connects school learning to personal life.

A Portfolio to Show Reflection and Self-Evaluation
Connects work to content criteria.
Evaluates work in light of criteria.
Identifies goals of future learning.

What makes these examples appropriate for a portfolio focus is that they describe the big ideas that are embedded in the curriculum. They define major goals of instruction over time, not just the focus for a day's lesson. For example, a first-grade teacher might select "the use of pictures, graphs, and objects to represent mathematical ideas" as an area of learning for a focus in a mathematics portfolio. From month to month, children will be learning new mathematical ideas and how to represent those ideas in a variety of ways. A simple drawing about the value of 5 in September will be offset by drawings to represent subtraction and addition facts in October and place value in March. As the use of pictures, graphs, and objects is explored with the study of different topics throughout the year, the intention is to develop an understanding of mathematical models and their use. The portfolio with student reflections is the ideal place to assess whether or not students grasp the big idea of mathematical models.

Teachers can use portfolios to target one dimension of performance in a subject area—for example, creative writing in language arts—but in some cases they might want to target more than one area. However, it is important for a teacher not to attempt to include too many different areas. When a teacher is using a portfolio to assess several areas of learning, it is best to have a common theme or learning goal that runs across the areas. For example, the ability to communicate is an area of learning considered important in many subject areas. Communication, then, might become a theme for a portfolio that covers several school subjects.

Step 2. Decide if the collection will be a showcase or a growth portfolio.

As we mentioned earlier, if the portfolio is to show growth over time, some initial pieces of work must be included to document a starting place. Teachers may want to keep particular pieces of work from the first two or three weeks of school or the beginning of a unit that are related to the area of learning in order to document what students could do initially. Students would then add pieces of work at different times during the course of instruction to demonstrate growth.

If a showcase format is preferred, then the collection of pieces primarily documents the students' best work. However, when the showcase collections from each report period are saved and reviewed with the new collection of work from the current reporting period, the progress students have made from reporting period to reporting period becomes obvious.

Thus it is possible for a portfolio to serve both purposes. This is why it is useful to select a focus for the collection that is broad enough to be an area of learning throughout the year.

Step 3. Decide on the physical form of the portfolio.

The physical form of the portfolio will be influenced by several factors. First, the teacher must decide how big the collection will be. Also, consideration should be given to the type of artifacts that are apt to be included in the collection. Finally, the teacher must think about availability of materials and storage space.

The size of a portfolio is directly dependent on its purpose. If, for example, the goal is a showcase portfolio of writing, a relatively small number of pieces would suffice. The collection might include a sample of the student's best writing for each of the genres studied. On the other hand, a growth portfolio would be larger because it would contain writing samples from different times during the year. If the purpose of the collection is also to demonstrate growth in the writing process, then drafts, revisions, and edited forms of at least some pieces of work would also be included. In general, a teacher should have some idea about how large the collection will be before beginning the portfolio process. Teachers could use a file folder if the collection is to include a relatively small number of pieces, but they might prefer binders, file boxes, or other containers to accommodate larger collections.

The type of artifacts in the collection will also influence its form. If teachers will include audio- or videotapes, they can put pages with pockets in a binder or use boxlike containers. In other cases oversized pieces in the collection—for example, drawings, pieces of art, science collections, or social studies projects—may require use of a special kind of container.

Some teachers use pizza boxes as portfolio containers for children's work. Local stores will often donate such materials to a school. One economical way to create a portfolio container is to use poster board to make a folder for student work. The poster board can be folded into sections (see Figure 6–3) to hold papers for up to three areas of learning.

Many teachers find that the types of work that truly illustrate the best of what children are learning may not fit in a file folder. For instance, in mathematics, children may glue beans on poster board to demonstrate understanding of place value or use blocks to show understanding of patterns. To document these types of work for the portfolios, some teachers make frequent use of cameras and even ask parents to contribute film and make donations for photo processing. Photos of class performances or of student presentations during show-and-tell and pictures of group projects can be included in a student's portfolio. Reflections on the back of each picture communicate the significance of the snapshot.

With the advent of electronic tools like digital cameras and specialized software it is possible for students to have electronic portfolios. The entire

To create the folder, first fold up the bottom 7 inches to form the pocket that will hold student papers. Next, from the left side fold 9⅓ inches to form one section of the folder. Repeat the fold from the right side. This will give you three sections with extra-deep pockets to hold regular-size and long pieces of paper. To personalize the portfolios, students can decorate the fronts and backs of the folders.

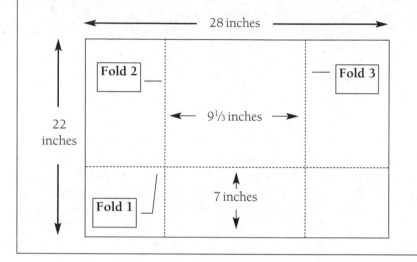

FIGURE 6–3   *Directions for creating a portfolio folder from poster board*

portfolio might be kept on a floppy disk. Teachers or students can use scanners to translate student work into electronic images. Students can develop their own homepages as their portfolios. Teachers must consider school district policies for acceptable use and issues related to student privacy and student/parent permissions before such student documents are actually put on a Web site. Yet development of an electronic portfolio will help students develop skills in the use of technology, organization, and communication. At the same time, the creation of a homepage can also provide a context to evaluate the development of technology skills. A videotape of a student performance or an audio representation of a student reading could be included if the capacity of the computer storage is adequate.

In most cases where portfolios work well, teachers provide storage for student work rather than expecting students to save work on their own over an extended period of time. When file folders are used, teachers can use drawers in file cabinets or plastic crates with hanging folders to save space. The crate technique makes it easy for the teacher to carry the set of folders to a teacher work room or home for examination. Obviously, large portfolio containers will take up more classroom space.

Step 4. Plan to incorporate the portfolio process into classroom activity.

Classrooms are busy places, and it is very easy for time to slip by without saving pieces of work that should be included in the portfolio. Teachers need to establish routines in their classrooms ensuring that students know the purpose of collecting work and how they should go about creating the portfolios. A process for saving artifacts as they are created and placing them in the working portfolio (see phase 2 of the "Portfolio Process" section) must be established in the classroom. It is essential to have a planned schedule of when students will select pieces of work. Teachers who schedule a regular time for students to examine and refine their working portfolios find that the final collections include pieces of work that provide useful information about student learning. Many try to have students examine their working portfolios every two or three weeks to clean them out.

The kind of activities that occur during the allocated portfolio time must be planned to help students develop the skill and insight needed to participate in the phases of the portfolio process described earlier. Teachers could plan classroom lessons in which they model how students should select artifacts. It's also helpful to schedule other activities that provide opportunities for a student to have a conversation about the collection and pieces in it. The teacher might plan times to conference with individual students about their working portfolios. As we mentioned earlier, such individual conferences are important opportunities to help students gain insights into the learning outcomes that should be documented.

At other times a teacher might plan time for students to work in groups to examine each student's collection and express opinions about why one piece of work should be saved and not another. Some teachers use math buddies or reading buddies from upper grade levels for certain activities in their classroom. Younger children might be asked to show and explain the pieces in their working portfolios to their buddies. The buddies might help younger children write comments about the pieces on cover sheets attached to each piece. A wide range of activities can be used to support the portfolio process, and teachers must plan to systematically include these events in the flow of daily schedules.

Step 5. Develop a strategy to evaluate the portfolio.

One of the reasons many teachers have difficulty with portfolio assessment is that they do not plan strategies to evaluate the portfolios before beginning to use this assessment approach. In some cases the teacher might try to evaluate each piece of work in the collection and add or average the separate grades. In such cases, the teacher often finds herself grading work that she already evaluated. A better approach is to plan a strategy that will result in assessing the work collectively. The following discussion assumes this latter approach will be used.

The evaluation may take different forms. In some cases, a grade, score, or proficiency label may be assigned. In others, the student and teacher review the collection and, based on their judgments about the work, set goals without explicitly assigning a grade, score, or label to the portfolio.

If the goal is to assign a grade, a scoring guide will be useful. See Chapter 4 for guidelines for developing scoring guides. The evaluative criteria must be related to the purpose of the portfolio. Imagine the use of a portfolio to assess students' problem-solving ability, especially with regard to their use of a variety of strategies when solving problems. The following evaluative criteria might be appropriate to assess student learning in this case:

- understanding and interpretation of different types of problems
- ability to find solutions and validate answers
- basic mathematics skill or knowledge
- ability to communicate explanations of strategies or approaches

When teachers develop documents such as the portfolio log (see Figure 6–2) or the preset table of contents (Figure 6–1), they communicate the evaluative criteria that will be considered in the assessment. For example, the elements of the writing process outlined in the writing portfolio log (Figure 6–2) would clearly be incorporated in the evaluative criteria for the portfolio rubric.

Typically the criteria to evaluate portfolios will focus on the big ideas, not the surface features of student work. If the portfolio is to effectively demonstrate a student's ability to solve complex problems or apply mathematics to unfamiliar situations, teachers would want the portfolio grade to be an index of that performance and would not assign a lower score because of random computational errors. When evaluative criteria demand perfection, students may focus on computational accuracy and select pieces of work that are less complex. In such cases, the depth and breadth of student learning might not be represented in the collection. Allowing students to edit papers when preparing their final portfolios for evaluation allows them to include whatever pieces they feel best represent their problem-solving ability. The edits will also demonstrate students' ability to find their own errors and make corrections.

The next decision is selecting an analytic or holistic approach to grading. One analytic approach, the checklist, can be developed to monitor the presence or absence of documentation of certain performances. For example, if a portfolio is to document students' ability to use computers, a checklist like the one in Figure 6–4 could be useful for the evaluation. Although the checklist acknowledges the presence of pieces of work documenting each skill, it does not take into account differences in the quality of student performance.

When assessing differences in the quality of performance is important, the teacher might prefer a point-allocated checklist or an analytic or a holistic rubric. The checklist in Figure 6–4 could become a point-allocated checklist by specifying the number of points that might be given for each item on the checklist. For example, the teacher might prefer to give one, two, or three points for the use of clip art, depending on the quality of student work. Teachers may also want to give more points for the skill areas that are more complex, such as the development of a homepage.

If the teachers is going to use rubrics in the evaluation, then she must write descriptors using either an analytic or a holistic approach. In the math example, an analytic (Figure 6–5) or a holistic approach (Figure 6–6) might be used to evaluate a portfolio. Use of an analytic rubric would provide students with a score for each area of learning.

The holistic rubric (Figure 6–6) assesses students' work considering almost the same characteristics as the previous analytic rubric. However, scoring with the holistic rubric will provide each student with only one score that reflects his or her overall performance. The holistic rubric in the example uses a five-point scale. We created an additional level at the top of the scale to introduce the components of creativity, use of atypical approaches, use of technology, and perseverance. The descriptors at Levels 3 and 4 are very much alike. Level 4 is characterized by dimensions of performance that go beyond those addressed in other levels of the rubric. This strategy allows the teacher to give special recognition to students who demonstrate talent in the work they included in the portfolio. Some find giving consideration to creativity questionable because it is not explicitly taught in most classrooms (Gredler 1999). At the same time, some teachers may feel that the identification of such characteristics encourages students to strive to attain them. When teachers identify such criteria as important, students

---

Name: **Date:**

Check   **Computer Skills**

_____   Uses a word-processing program.
_____   Uses a spreadsheet.
_____   Incorporates clip art in documents.
_____   Makes graphs and tables from spreadsheet.
_____   Uses e-mail.
_____   Conducts a Web search using a search engine.
_____   Downloads software off the Web.
_____   Creates a homepage.

FIGURE 6–4   *Computer skills checklist*

Understanding and Interpretation

Level 3   Work shows clear understanding of problem situations. The student uses given information that is important and disregards extraneous information.

Level 2   Work shows understanding of problem situations. The student may misuse or ignore given information that is important or may use information that is extraneous.

Level 1   Work shows little understanding of questions implied by problem situations and important information is ignored or used inappropriately.

Level 0   No attempt to do the problem.

Ability to Find Solutions and Validate the Answer

Level 3   Work consistently shows the ability to select appropriate strategies (even though occasional computational errors may occur). Also, the student checks work or writes a rationale showing how the answer fits the conditions.

Level 2   Either an inappropriate strategy is selected or the student does not check work and justify the answer in light of the context.

Level 1   Student selects inappropriate strategies and does not check work or discuss the validity of the answer.

Level 0   No attempt to do the problem.

Basic Mathematics Skill or Knowledge

Level 3   Correct interpretation of mathematics terms is apparent and computational errors are rare and have been edited.

Level 2   Frequent computational errors, most of which have been edited, or selections do not show knowledge of mathematical terms.

Level 1   Frequent mathematical errors, which have not been edited or have been incorrectly edited.

Level 0   No attempt to do the problem.

Ability to Communicate Explanations of Strategies or Approaches

Level 3   Some work shows ability to explain the procedures that were used and provides a rationale for the decision to use these procedures.

Level 2   Student offers explanations of the procedure used and the rationale for this choice of the approach but the explanation is vague and may have minor errors.

Level 1   Student work does not demonstrate use of communication skills related to procedures and rationale or those that are presented are incorrect and difficult to follow.

Level 0   No attempt to do the problem.

(adapted from Kuhs 1997)

FIGURE 6–5   *Analytic rubric for problem-solving portfolio*

Proficiency Levels	Descriptions
Level 4	Across problem-solving situations, student work shows clear understanding of what is being asked, using given information appropriately. Work consistently shows the ability to select appropriate strategies. Correct interpretation of mathematics terms is apparent and computational errors are rare and have been edited. The ability to explain the procedures that were used and provide a rationale for the decision to use these procedures is demonstrated. In addition, at least one of the following characteristics distinguishes the Level 4 portfolio: • evidence of creative or insightful, but atypical, approaches to problems; • use of technology in either the presentation or solution of a problem; and • perseverance and tenacity in dealing with complexity, obscurity, or ambiguity.
Level 3	Across problem-solving situations, student work shows clear understanding of what is being asked, using given information appropriately. Work consistently shows the ability to select appropriate strategies. Correct interpretation of mathematics terms is apparent and computational errors are rare and have been edited. The ability to explain the procedures that were used and provide a rationale for the decision to use these procedures is demonstrated.
Level 2	Across problem-solving situations, student work generally shows an understanding of what is being asked, but the student may misuse or ignore given information. In some cases the work shows the ability to select appropriate strategies but unedited computational errors or misinterpreted terms are apparent. The student attempts to explain the use of procedures and provide a rationale for their use.
Level 1	Across problem-solving situations, student work generally shows little understanding of what is being asked. The student may misuse or ignore given information. The ability to select appropriate strategies is not evident. Unedited computational errors or misinterpreted terms are apparent. Explanations of procedures and rationales lack clarity or are not provided.
Level 0	Portfolio is incomplete or contains no work meeting the descriptions above.

(adapted from Kuhs 1997)

FIGURE 6–6 *Holistic rubric for problem-solving portfolio*

may begin looking for opportunities to be creative or to show talent in working with technology.

POWER AND PURPOSE OF PORTFOLIOS

Portfolios are good assessment approaches but they are labor intensive. Thus, portfolio assessment should only be used when it has the potential to provide better understandings about student learning than other assessment approaches. A teacher can assess the ability of the portfolio to accomplish this by asking, "What is it I want to know about student learning that I cannot find out in another way? What can a portfolio tell about student learning that cannot be told by a single performance task?"

Clearly, in the case of a growth portfolio, the collection of student work shows the development of skills and understandings that has occurred over the period documented by the portfolio, something a single task cannot do. Such growth evidence is especially useful when teaching exceptional learners. With those who have learning difficulties, performance on particular tasks as compared to the performance of their peers may lead one to ask, when looking at a single piece of work late in the year, "Did this student benefit in any way from instruction?" At the same time, each piece of work by a highly gifted student is typically at such a high level of performance that, looking at a piece of work late in the year, a teacher might again ask: "Did this student benefit in any way from instruction this year?" When a growth portfolio is available, the learning that has occurred can be confirmed by contrasting a student's performance on earlier pieces of work with the most recent ones. This is true for exceptional learners and others as well.

Another benefit of a portfolio approach to assessment is that it provides a holistic picture of student learning. With either a growth or a showcase portfolio, the reviewer can observe a student's synthesis of disparate tasks into the big ideas of the curriculum. For example, during the school year students may complete a series of tasks in science class related to systems. Achievement standards for this area of study are outlined in the first column of Figure 6–7. Activities to assess performance related to these standards are in the second column. As shown in the figure, the student work related to Standard C would demonstrate the student's level of insight into how a missing element affects other system components. In another task (Standard D), the student's ability to recognize subsystems would be in evidence. The assessment question "How deep is the student's understanding of the concept of *system*?" could be answered by considering whether the student's integrative statement conceptualizes systems as being composed of parts, functions, subsystems, and interactions. In other words, is the child able to integrate all this information into the big idea of systems?

Portfolios also facilitate communication about students' learning with family members, next year's teacher, or others. Teachers and administrators share a common professional language that is often unclear and intimidating to parents. When parents review a portfolio of actual student work, they see a clear illustration of what a student has accomplished. For example, a portfolio containing a story that a student wrote early in the year and one written much later is a concrete record of how the student's writing ability has developed. After reviewing examples of students' work in the collections, the next year's teacher will gain insight into what students studied during the previous year and an individual's accomplishments and limitations. The new teacher can then build on previous learning. For administrators, the portfolio documents the types of work students are experiencing and reveals their level of success.

Portfolio use also has the potential to affect students' development as lifelong learners. As students talk about their collections and share ideas, they develop the independence that will be important for future academic success. Students learn from looking at other people's work. Even students who usually have perfect papers will benefit from seeing how others use descriptive language to describe characters, how they alternate frequently used words with synonyms, and how they select words to establish mood in a story. When students have opportunities to see the kind of work others do, they have models for improving themselves.

Achievement Standards Related to the Study of Systems[1]	Activities
A. Know that most things are made of parts.	Students are asked to describe the form and function of a clip-type clothespin to someone who has never seen one.[2]
B. Know that in something that consists of many parts, the parts usually influence one another.	A class identifies the purposes of different living and nonliving things in their aquarium.
C. Something may not work as well (or at all) if a part of it is missing, broken, worn out, mismatched, or misconnected.	When studying plants, students will identify the parts of an ecosystem and manipulate one part of a system (e.g., water, light, heat) to determine essential elements.
D. Any system is usually connected to other systems, both internally and externally. Thus a system may be thought of as containing subsystems and as being a subsystem of a larger system.	After examining a flashlight, students are asked to "list the components necessary for a common flashlight according to the systems involved."[3]
[1]from American Association for the Advancement of Science (1993, 264–65) [2]from Ebert and Ebert (1998, 73) [3]from Ebert and Ebert (1998, 8)	

FIGURE 6–7 *Standards and activities for the study of systems*

Graded assignments and homework take on new significance for the child who is thinking about the need for a good paper for the portfolio. Consideration of low-achieving students' approach to daily work suggests that they may not recognize daily or routine classroom activity as important to their learning. When pieces of daily work are potential entries for the showcase portfolio, students come to see that daily work is important. In this way the portfolio process can guide learners to be more effective students as they start paying attention to all opportunities to learn.

7 | INTERVIEWS
Classroom Conversations to Assess Learning

An assessment interview is a one-on-one conversation between teacher and student with the purpose of developing insight into what the student has learned. Such an interview is one of many conversations that occur in the classrooms between a teacher and the students. The brief exchange between teacher and student while the teacher is monitoring independent student work might be considered an informal assessment interview, but this chapter will focus only on those occasions when a teacher formally engages a student in a conversation for the purpose of assessment. Many have found such interviews to be an important assessment tool for some students in some situations.

The interview presents an excellent opportunity to assess student understandings and abilities that cannot be assessed in other ways. Sometimes a student's work on a written assessment seems inconsistent with classroom performance. The interview presents an opportunity to ask the reason for such inconsistency. Some learners may have difficulty processing oral information. Others may have reading difficulty, that is, their problem is an inability to interpret written text. Still others may understand the written text, or read the oral prompt, but have difficulty communicating their responses in a particular format. More generally, the teacher wants to know how well the student received the information, how he deals with the information, how he connects it to other ideas already learned, and how he communicates a response to the information (Feuerstein et al. 1987). Interviews provide the opportunity to assess these important process skills.

Imagine a fourth-grade teacher who has just taught students the rules for starting new paragraphs in fictional writing. After the lesson, she asked students to write stories and to use their newly learned rules to put paragraphs in the correct places. Much to the teacher's chagrin, several students did not use paragraphs in their stories. The teacher wonders why the students did not use the rules that the class had discussed. Following the above schema, the teacher might ask herself: Was the difficulty that the students did not remember the rules? Did they remember them, but not know how to apply them to their own writing? Were there other writing difficulties that got in the way of them using paragraph structure in their writing? An interview would be a good way to assess the cause of student difficulty with paragraphing.

ELEMENTS OF AN INTERVIEW

In planning an assessment interview, the teacher must take certain key elements into consideration. Central elements to an interview are the student and teacher. The conversation between these individuals, in the form of questions and answers, produces new understandings of the student's thought processes and how these processes influence what she knows and is able to do.

To guide the interview, the teacher should think about the conversation ahead of time and prepare a set of notes called an interview protocol to ensure that he will present tasks to the student in a clear manner and that he will cover important questions. The interview protocol is made up of prompts—questions, tasks, or directive statements—which will indicate what the student is to do. In addition, the protocol contains directions for the teacher to follow during the interview. These teacher directions include instructions about materials and how they might be used in the interview as well as cues to probe further when students make certain responses. Sometimes the prompts will involve the use of certain materials such as previous assessments, pieces of work, or other items that are commonly used for instruction, such as blocks, counters, scales, paper, markers, calculators, diagrams, and the like.

During an interview it is important to be sure the student understands what you are asking. As we mentioned earlier, some students have difficulty processing oral information, while others may have difficulty reading problem statements. For this reason it is useful to consider whether to give the problems and prompts in oral or written form.

In planning the interview, a teacher must also consider the structure of the interview, the level of interaction between teacher and student, the strategy for recording student responses such as audiotape or written notes, the time and place for the interview, and a method for evaluating student responses. All of these elements are addressed in the following sections.

Structured and unstructured interviews

In the chapter on performance assessment we talked about whether a performance task is structured or unstructured. The same idea is useful in thinking about interviews; interviews can be more or less structured, depending on the purpose and the complexity of the content to be assessed. In a highly structured interview the teacher gives more explicit direction about the expected response than in an unstructured one. The directions may lead the student through a problem in a sequential manner or address a series of concepts and skills in an orderly fashion.

Notice the interview with Olivia below. The teacher engaged the student in a problem-solving activity that was designed to assess understanding of the significance of place value. She did not, however, merely give Olivia a problem and ask her to work on it. Rather, the teacher asked her a series of questions that led to a solution of the problem and, at the same time, engaged Olivia in a conversation about place value.

Teacher: Imagine you are working at a bakery and this is your first day on the job. Let's pretend these counters are hamburger buns. *(The teacher puts twenty-three counters on the table.)* How many buns do you have?

Olivia *(Begins counting by twos):* Two, four, six, . . . twenty, twenty-two, twenty-three.

Teacher: Please write this number on the paper.
(Olivia writes 23.)

Teacher: I see that you wrote two symbols, a two and a three. In twenty-three, which symbol stands for more buns?

Olivia: The three.

Teacher: Suppose the baker asks you to package the buns, ten in a bag. How many bags do you think you will need?
(Olivia does not respond—looking from the counters to the window, fidgeting.)

Teacher: Tell me what you are thinking, Olivia.

Olivia: I don't know what to do.

Teacher: Why don't you start by counting out some for the first bag.
(Olivia begins counting by twos and stops at ten.)

Teacher: OK, that's one bag. Now what would you do?

Olivia: Count out another one?

Teacher: Yes, go ahead, do it.
(Olivia counts out ten more and looks at the teacher.)

Teacher: OK, how many bags do you need?

Olivia: Two.

Teacher: Did all your buns fit in the two bags?

Olivia: No, these three were left.

Teacher: Let's look back at the number you wrote to tell how many buns you had.

Olivia: Twenty-three.

Teacher: How do your counters show what the two represents?

Olivia: I have two groups of ten, that's two in the tens place.

Teacher: And the three?

Olivia: These three extra buns.

Teacher: OK, now, which represents more buns, the two or the three?

The strength of the structured approach is that it allows the teacher to control the conversation, being sure that the particular concepts that he's assessing are used by the students. For example, doing the bun problem, Olivia would not have thought about place value. The teacher used structured questions to assess Olivia's understanding of that concept.

If the goal had been to assess problem-solving strategies, an unstructured interview might have been best. The advantage of the unstructured interview is that the student must bring his understanding of the problem to the situation. In other words, it allows the teacher to understand if the student is able to marshal the important concepts for the solution of a problem or to transfer learned concepts from a similar problem to a new situation.

Using an unstructured approach with the bakery problem, a teacher might tell the story and ask the student how many packages of ten buns she could make. The challenge of the bakery problem almost disappears in the highly structured interview. In an unstructured approach, the integrity of the problem is preserved, but the student may or may not reveal knowledge of place value, depending on the way she solves problem. Thus, an interview with less structure gives the teacher less control over the content of the interview, but greater understanding of how students interpret situations and apply their knowledge.

Less structured interviews also allow questions that play off the context of the conversation. For example, a science teacher might want to gain insight into a child's understanding of the change of seasons. The interviewer might begin simply by asking, "What causes the change in seasons?" The intention is to allow the student to organize a response and communicate everything that seems relevant. If the student drifts in the response and begins talking about the characteristics of seasons, for example, saying something like, "In winter it gets cold," rather than describing the causes, the teacher would be prepared to redirect the conversation by saying, "Why do you think that happens?" Notice that this second question plays off the student's response and therefore could not be preplanned. While interviewing a different student, the teacher may not even ask this question if the student's response gets to the heart of the intended topic of conversation without probing.

Typically, when teachers decide to interview students, it is useful to give thought to the level of structure that will accommodate the purpose. Greater structure allows the teacher to direct student responses to cover each concept, principle, or generalization that might be of interest in the assessment. In a highly unstructured interview, the teacher has less control of the flow of the response and one must be careful when making inferences about student responses.

As we mentioned earlier, when addressing the bakery problem in an unstructured interview, a student may never mention place value because she used another strategy and there was no need to think about place value; in another case a student may get sidetracked and forget to mention it. In either case it would be impossible to make judgments about the student's understanding of place value. For this reason it is always useful for the teacher to have a list of key concepts or ideas that are to be assessed in the interview. Toward the end of an interview session, the teacher may want to ask explicit questions about concepts that were on the list if the student never mentioned them. The teacher should do this whether the interview is structured or unstructured because, if a concept were not mentioned, the teacher cannot assume the student does not know it.

Traditional and instructional interviews

The manner in which an interview is conducted lies along a continuum from traditional to instructional. In a traditional interview, a teacher asks a student a series of questions, notes the responses, and gives little or no feedback. The traditional interview provides a snapshot of a learner's knowledge at a given time. When conducting such an interview, a teacher typically avoids questions or prompts that might be seen as hints. The goal in such an interview is to determine what a student knows and can do independently, without assistance. Teachers may use this approach with learners who, for some reason, cannot demonstrate what they know through other assessments.

The instructional interview serves both an assessment and instructional purpose. In such cases, a teacher provides prompts during the interview to guide or correct the student responses. These prompts may be merely clues or hints, or they may actually be instructional statements. Vygotsky (1978) proposed that the teacher should interact with the student during an assessment to maximize the appraisal of student knowledge and ability. His concept of the *zone of proximal development* explains the difference between what the student can achieve independently and what the student will achieve if given prompts or hints. Within an instructional interview, a teacher determines the level of work a student can do independently. Then, using progressive hints in the interview, the teacher explores the zone of proximal development and gains insight into the knowledge or understandings the student is able to construct with limited or minimal coaching. The teacher also learns which concepts present the student with difficulty and will require more intensive instruction. Consider the following assessment interview:

Teacher: Name a four-sided figure.
  Harry: A rectangle.
Teacher: Can you name one that is not a parallelogram?
  Harry: A rhombus.
Teacher: Do you remember when we called a rhombus a diamond shape?
  Harry: Yes.
Teacher: Are the opposite sides parallel in a rhombus?
  Harry: Ohhh, what is the name for that shape? (*Harry moves his hands in the air and traces a trapezoid.*)
Teacher: It starts with a *t*.
  Harry: Trapezoid!

Note that the teacher provided direct instruction when prompting the student, "Do you remember when we called a rhombus a diamond shape?"

Later in the conversation, Harry still could not recall the term *trapezoid* and the teacher gave a clue, saying, "It starts with a *t*."

Sometimes in an instructional interview, a student response identifies something the learner does not know or remember, but can easily master with only a little assistance. In the previous interview, Harry did not recognize that if opposite sides are parallel, the shape is a parallelogram. He said a rhombus was not a parallelogram. The teacher provided instruction by reminding him that a rhombus has a diamond shape and asking if opposite sides are parallel in a diamond. In response, Harry demonstrated that, with little assistance, he could develop an understanding of the characteristics of a parallelogram. He showed his understanding by tracing a shape that was not a parallelogram in the air. With further prompting the teacher learned that Harry knew the term *trapezoid* and could relate it to the figure he was tracing with some coaching.

In an instructional interview the teacher poses an initial question or problem and, if the student's independent response is flawed, subsequent dialog may seem almost like a coaching session in which the teacher cues the student to try new approaches, rethink an answer, or extend an idea from a previous example. The level of interaction between teacher and student is a defining element on the continuum of interview types.

Feuerstein et al. (1987) suggest the interviewer should be a teacher/observer and the student a learner/observer. The interviewer observes responses, and then intervenes as appropriate, making remarks and asking for or providing explanations. For example, when asked, "What is the cause of the seasons of the year?" a student might say, "The Earth is farther away from the Sun in winter." In an instructional approach, a possible follow-up to this incorrect response might be to have the student look at a diagram that labels the seasons at various points in the Earth's orbit around the Sun. The teacher might remark, "Hmmm, that does not seem to fit this drawing. Here it looks like the Earth is actually closer to the Sun in the winter than in the summer. Do you remember what we said about this in class?"

Such a response cues the student to a classroom conversation about the phenomenon being assessed. The student then might be able to back off the original statement and, recalling the lesson about seasons, correct the response by saying, "Oh yeah, it is the angle that makes the difference. In summer the Earth gets direct rays and that makes it hot." As illustrated here, during an instructional interview, the teacher provides more explicit cues and hints in order to gain a better understanding of student knowledge and to assess the need for further instruction.

PURPOSE OF ASSESSMENT INTERVIEWS

Sometimes the purpose of interviewing is to provide information that will allow the teacher to make an accurate interpretation of a student's responses to other types of assessment completed earlier. In the case of a first-grade student whose writing is merely a series of letters, mostly consonants, one might conclude the child has not learned to write meaningfully. The teacher might ask the student who wrote, "Mi S tr Lik Kn D," to read the sentence. The child might say, "My sister likes candy," showing that what seemed to be random letters are really connected to the sounds of the sentence that he wanted to write. The oral communication during the interview provides important information about what the child knows and is able to do.

Imagine a student, Luisa, who is having difficulty drawing conclusions based on information that is presented in graphic form. The teacher has observed this in classroom discussions and in her journal entries. The sample multiple-choice problem from Chapter 5 (Figure 5–3) is meant to assess students' ability to read and interpret information from graphs and draw conclusions. Perhaps this item was on a social studies quiz and Luisa missed it. The teacher might interview Luisa using the protocol on the next page to evaluate her ability related to this area of learning. As shown in Figure 7–1, during an interview, the teacher might use the graphs from the multiple-choice item as a prompt to explore student understanding and make judgments about the student's responses. The checklist in Figure 7–2 could be used to create a record of the performance.

STEPS IN PLANNING AN ASSESSMENT INTERVIEW

As was the case in other chapters, it is difficult to outline the steps for planning an interview, implying that they proceed one after the other. Once again, the planning occurs in an iterative fashion so that a choice at one level affects decisions made later and vice versa. We only attempt to offer the following steps as a strategy to ensure that you give all important decisions appropriate consideration.

Step 1. Identify students whom you might want to interview.

The decision about how many and which students to interview is very important. Assessment interviews, like portfolios, are time intensive and should be used when there is a potential to provide insight into student learning that cannot be gained in other ways. Particular situations where student interviews might be useful include:

- when a student's literacy skills limit the quality of written communication
- when a new student joins a class during the year
- when disabilities such as attention deficit disorder negatively affect performance on other assessments
- when students have had a particularly difficult time with previous assessments
- when student performance on an assignment or test is dramatically inconsistent with expectations based on past performance

Look at the two graphs on your paper.

1. What conclusion could you reach using these two graphs?

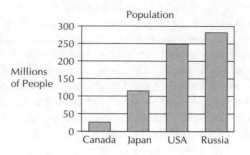
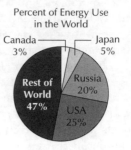

2. What are these two graphs about?
   - What are the titles?
   - What does the first graph tell about energy use?
   - Why are the pie pieces different sizes?
   - What do the numbers around the circle tell you?
   - How much of the world's energy did the USA use?
   - What does the graph tell us about the energy use of other countries?
   - Let's make a chart. List the percent of energy use for each country.

Country	Energy Use	
Canada		
Japan		
USA		
Russia		

   - What does the second graph tell about the population?
   - What are the labels on the bottom?
   - What do the numbers along the side mean?
   - What is the population of each country?
   - Put the population for each country in the table.

Country	Energy Use	Population
Canada		
Japan		
USA		
Russia		

3. What conclusion could you reach using the information on these two graphs?

FIGURE 7–1   *Questions for a social studies interview*

Student Name:		Date:
✔	Performances	Teacher Notes
	Identifies elements within a graph (i.e., legend, title, labels, and axes).	
	Reads information from the graph.	
	Draws conclusions based on information from a single graph.	
	Integrates information from more than one source (table, graph, diagram).	

FIGURE 7–2 *Interview checklist*

Step 2. Select a focus for the interview and draft a content outline.

For the most part, the teacher has a general notion of the content he will address when he identifies the student. If a student's performance were questionable on another assessment, the content focus of an interview would be defined by the previous assessment. For instance, in a social studies essay exam on which students were expected to discuss a foreign conflict from the point of view of a citizen of another nation, a student may not have addressed all the dimensions of the issue. The follow-up interview, therefore, would focus on social studies, and in particular, the student's awareness of the matters that were overlooked in the written assessment.

In the case of a student's apparent lack of understanding of how to calculate the area of polygons, the teacher may want to interview her to develop an understanding of the reason for the difficulty. Thus the interview would target the mathematics content that has been a problem or certain areas of prerequisite understanding. At this stage the teacher should create an outline of student performances or understandings to assess. The following list is a teacher's draft of content that will be the focus of an assessment interview for the student having difficulty with the concept of area. Frequently teachers use textbooks or curriculum guides when drafting such outlines.

Initial Outline of Focus for an Interview About Area of Polygons

1. Determine if student can find the area of regular and irregular polygons by counting (using concrete and pictorial models).

2. Determine how a student finds area of rectangular shapes when given dimensions (with and without drawings).
3. Determine if the student knows and can use a formula to find area when given dimensions of rectangular shapes with and without drawings.
4. If the student has trouble with formula use, determine whether the difficulty is with the concept of area or with multiplication skills.
5. Determine if the student can see and use the concept of area in applied contexts.

Step 3. Decide the level of structure needed in the interview and draft some questions.

In planning an interview about how to find the area of polygons with a student who has experienced difficulty, a semistructured approach might be useful. The teacher may want to begin by giving an open-ended task and asking the student to talk about what she is doing, a strategy sometimes referred to as a think-aloud. Yet, certain basic understandings are essential to success in finding area, and the teacher may need to structure explicit questions or prompts in order to reveal the student's level of understanding of that content. Such prompts drafted for an interview about the area of polygons (see Figure 7–3) were developed from the content outline drafted in Step 2. The italicized words provide directions for the teacher to follow as he conducts the interview. The content code beside each prompt shows which topic in the initial outline is related to the question.

Step 4. Decide the level of interaction—traditional or instructional.

The decision about how much interaction and how many prompts or hints are appropriate in an interview is connected to the purpose of the interview. If the goal is to conduct an assessment that provides a snapshot of the student's independent functioning at a point in time, the traditional approach is preferable. If, however, the teacher wants an assessment that serves both an assessment purpose and an instructional one, the teacher should use instructional prompts, hints, and questions to guide or correct the student responses during the interview.

In Figure 7–3, content code 4 relates to an instance when a student can't use a formula to find the area of a rectangle. In such a case, the interviewer would want to know if the student did not understand use of formulas in general, if the problem were merely with multiplication skills, or if it were some other underlying problem. At this stage the teacher might want to begin with prompts that are not instructional. If the student gave no response when asked to use the formula, the interviewer might ask, "What do you need to do first?" A student who knows about formulas would say, "Put six in for l and three in for w." A student who did not know about formulas could not say this and might not give a response or might give an inappropriate response.

Content Code	Prompts
1	a) *The teacher gives the student a geoboard with a 3-by-4 rectangle represented and says,* I'd like you to find the area of the shape on this geoboard. Tell me what you are thinking and doing as you find the area. b) *After the student responds and teacher probes (if necessary), the teacher puts an irregular polygon on the geoboard and asks,* Now, can you find the area of this shape?
2	a) *The teacher shows the student a drawing of a rectangle labeled 5 cm and 7 cm and says,* Find the area of this shape. As you are doing the problem, tell me how you are finding the area. b) *The teacher writes "6 in." and "8 in." on a sheet of paper, saying,* Find the area of a rectangle that has a length of six inches and a width of eight inches. Remember to think out loud as you solve the problem.
3	a) *If the student used the formula area = l × w in number 2a or 2b, skip this question. If not, ask,* What formula can be used to find the area of a rectangle? b) *Show the student a drawing of a rectangle labeled with length of 6 cm and width of 3 cm and say,* Use the formula area = l × w to find the area of this rectangle. Remember to talk out loud as you solve the problem.
4	a) *If student has trouble using the formula, use probes to determine the possible reason(s) for difficulty. (See Step 4 about probes.)*
5	a) *Show the student the following problem as you read it:* Benny had to paint the wall of his bedroom when he took his old posters down. The wall is 9 feet high and 10 feet long with no windows or doors on it. Benny wants to know whether he should buy one quart of paint or whether he'll need more (1 quart of paint will cover 100 square feet). How much paint do you think Benny will need? Remember to think out loud as you figure out how much paint he will need.

FIGURE 7–3   *Draft of interview prompts on area of polygons*

For the student who knew about the substitution, the interviewer might ask, "And what do you do next?" Through such repeated questioning, the teacher would see where the breakdown in student knowledge or ability occurs. Such noninstructional probes help reveal areas of student difficulty without teaching new ideas or procedures to the student.

A distinguishing characteristic of an instructional interview is that the probes become hintlike. The probes are actually cues for the student to think about something that she may have ignored, to rethink an answer, or to try a different approach. In an instructional interview, the follow-up probes and cues are planned in a manner that begins with simple cues and moves on to progressively stronger hints, ultimately teaching the student how to respond.

Returning to the example of the student who couldn't use a formula to find the area of a rectangle, in an instructional interview the teacher might still ask, "What do you need to do first?" For the student who did not respond, the teacher might offer a cue by reminding the student of a previous lesson, asking, "What did we do with formulas like this yesterday in class?" If there is no response, the teacher might provide a hint by asking, "What do the l and w stand for?" Successive cues that provide increasing levels of assistance would include:

What was the length of the rectangle in this problem? The width?
If you put the length in for l and the width in for w, what does the formula tell you to do next?
What do you get for an answer?

Once again, the repeated questioning allows the teacher to see where the breakdown in student knowledge or ability occurs. However, in this case, the student may be learning the skills needed to solve the problem. At some point along the way, perhaps after being cued to substitute values for letters, or perhaps after being cued to multiply, the student may be able to proceed without further coaching. In the case of a student who had to be coached through most of the task, the teacher should be prepared to give the student another problem that will reveal whether the student has now learned to do the work independently or if further instruction is needed.

Sample probes and cues are provided in the following lists. Those listed as probes would be appropriate for either a traditional or an instructional interview. The cues are typically used only for instructional interviews but, if a student is having real difficulty and little is being accomplished in a traditional interview, such cues may be used. The teacher must bear in mind that as the level of interaction increases, the amount of information we gain about a student's independent understanding decreases.

Probes

What do you think you should do first?
Please tell me more about that.
Show me how you got that answer.
Tell me why you think that is the answer.
Was there a rule you were following when you did that? Tell me which rule.
Can you do that another way? What would that be?

Draw a picture that shows that idea.
What do you do when you run into a problem you can't solve?
What do you do when you run into a word you don't know?

Cues

How is this similar to another problem we have seen?
How is this part of the story like a part that we read earlier?
Does this answer seem reasonable?
What did we learn about reading the lines of a poem?
Would you restate the question in your own words?
What should you do as you get ready to read a story?

Step 5. Plan a strategy to record responses.

When planning to record student responses, a teacher has a wide range of options: tape or video recordings, checklists, rubrics, or anecdotal records. Some provide more accurate records of the student responses, while others are more manageable and efficient. The teacher should base this decision on the content being assessed, how the assessment is to be used, and the resources and time that are available for the assessment.

An audio- or videotape of an interview captures the actual student performance and would be especially useful to assess some skills and understandings. Bentley, Ebert, and Ebert (2000) describe the use of interviews to assess student understanding of concepts in science. If the teacher collects tape recordings of such interviews over time, she can compare a student's initial understandings about science concepts with his statements in later interviews. Such a comparison may provide dramatic evidence of the change in student understanding. An advantage of such records is that they can be shared with parents and used to provide concrete examples to support the praise or concern a teacher wants to share about a student's progress in school. A disadvantage is that listening to tape recordings or viewing videotapes requires a considerable amount of time when a teacher is reviewing such assessments for a class of twenty students.

Anecdotal records (Harrington et al. 1997) or other notes taken by the teacher during the interview are less structured. When keeping such notes, teachers can use different formats. The types of notes described in Chapter 2 are often used for recording responses during an interview. A teacher might merely decide to write phrases or sentences that describe what the student says or does during the interview. These can be very detailed or cursory. If a teacher uses phrases or brief sentences, she will want to expand the narrative soon after the interview so that she doesn't lose the richness of the conversation.

Teachers may also use checklists or rubrics to provide a record of an interview, as illustrated in Figure 7–2. A checklist is especially useful when there is a series of predictable misunderstandings or errors or a set of basic understandings that the teacher will assess. The checklists and rubrics in

Chapter 4 can be adapted for use in recording the levels of understanding that a student demonstrates in an interview. For example, the rubric on communication in mathematics (Figure 4–6) could be a useful guide to evaluate performance in a mathematics interview.

Another method for creating a record for the interview is to write a student's responses on the protocol instead of using a checklist. In other instances the teacher might use a copy of the student's old work, such as a math test, a science lab report, or a journal entry, to record the student's interview responses about that work.

Step 6. Gather materials that will be useful during the interview.

Teachers can make best use of the time set aside for interviewing by gathering all materials in advance. The interview protocol will identify materials that must be available when conducting the session. For example, in the interview with the student about area, a geoboard with rubber bands is needed, as well as pencil and paper. In the case of an instructional interview, a teacher may want curriculum materials at hand such as texts, pictures, computers, pieces of student work, or any other item that might be useful to illustrate an idea or stimulate student thinking. In addition, equipment or materials for recording student responses should be ready before the session begins.

When the teacher is going to present a lengthy problem, he may first read the problem to the student without showing it in print. This strategy will allow the teacher to gauge whether the student is able to process oral information. If the student has difficulty understanding or remembering the information given orally, the teacher should give her a written copy of the problem. Even after the teacher presents the problem in written form, he may want to read it aloud again.

At other times the teacher will want to first give the student the written copy of the problem and have the student read it without assistance. This would provide an assessment of the student's ability to gather information from written text. When students are to read such printed materials, it is important to have such written copy prepared in advance in the correct print size and form for the student's age level.

Step 7. Determine where and when the interview will occur.

The timing of an interview is very important. The teacher should schedule the interview at a time when the entire conversation can be completed without distraction. The teacher might conduct an interview with one student at a table in the back of the room while the rest of the class is engaged in other work. It is important to have some level of privacy so that the student does not feel that other students are observing him. Yet, doing the interview during recess or a study hall could dramatically affect results. If the student resents the loss of free time, he may be preoccupied or rush through responses, not truly revealing what he knows and is able to do.

The teacher should strive to make the student comfortable if the interview is to be successful. As we mentioned earlier, the selection of time and place will affect the student's comfort level and perhaps her performance. Thinking of the interview as a conversation leads to interactions between the teacher and student that are apt to relax the student. You might begin by talking about recent school events or asking about a student's out-of-school interests. Introducing a playful element into the conversation might also put the student at ease. For example, in an interview about real and imaginary writing, the teacher might ask what Paddington Bear wears. She might follow up this question with a question about whether bears at the zoo wear raincoats. The hope is that the child would find this amusing and be relaxed as the teacher proceeds with other questions.

Once the student is comfortable, the interview can begin. If the teacher knows that the student is apt to have difficulty with the questions, it may be good to begin with some easy questions about the subject. Once the student has some level of comfort and confidence, the teacher can proceed with the questions outlined in the protocol. During the interview the teacher should be careful to give the student enough time to think and to respond. It may sometimes feel awkward when neither the student nor the teacher is talking, but such wait time is an important part of any classroom conversation. One hallmark of a good interview is that the student talks more than the teacher does.

If the student seems to be experiencing frustration or is distracted, the teacher might use probes to guide or redirect the student's thinking. An interviewer should be a careful listener. Follow-up questions and probes that are connected to the student's responses will show that the teacher is listening and values what the student has to say. Teachers should probe after both correct and incorrect answers. If a teacher only asks questions after a student has made a mistake, the student will be cued that he has made a mistake each time a teacher probes. This may make the student unsure of himself, and he may become uneasy as the interview progresses. Also, by probing after correct answers, the teacher can see if the student knows the appropriate strategies and essential content or is only making lucky guesses.

EVALUATION OF STUDENT RESPONSES

In most cases, teachers are not likely to assign a grade or score for an interview. Throughout this chapter the interview has been described as an assessment strategy that teachers are apt to use with some students in some situations, rather than an assessment done with every student. When interviews are used to explore the depth and breadth of student knowledge prior to instruction, the assessment is more likely to be seen as a tool for teacher planning than an evaluation that should be graded. While labels such as "Science project" or "Quiz 1" are likely to appear in a teacher's grade book, rarely would a column in a grade book be labeled "The interview."

At the same time, an interview performance may sometimes lead the teacher to modify her judgments about student learning. This would be true if, for example, an instructional interview focused on previous work on which the student experienced difficulty. Imagine that, after some initial coaching in the interview, the student was able to do similar work independently without assistance. In such a case the teacher may conclude that the student is now able to demonstrate the knowledge and ability that was assessed in the original work. The teacher may want to adjust the grade on the initial assessment to accurately reflect the student's current level of performance.

Should the student's grade on past work be changed? Should additional points be added because of the interview performance? If the student had done poorly on the interview, would points be taken away? When a student interview has been strong, the addition of points to a student's cumulative grade can be easily justified. The grade is supposed to be an indicator of what the student knows and can do. The additional points would be a correction to the inaccurate measure of learning from the previous work. If a student did not earn five points because she did not seem to understand one idea on the previous work, the teacher might add five points after the student demonstrated understanding during the interview. The use of a checklist can provide a basis for determining the number of points that might be added to a student's grade.

Subtraction of points, on the other hand, might not be fair. The student's score on previous work has already indicated a deficiency in knowledge. In this instance the interview merely affirms the accuracy of the previous assessment, and subtracting points might inappropriately exaggerate the deficiency. A parallel situation would deal with extra credit. A teacher might think it is appropriate to add points for an extra-credit assignment. We doubt that anyone would subtract points if performance on an extra-credit assignment were weak.

Clearly different teachers have different points of view about how much such interviews should influence report card grades. We feel, however, that a student's performance during the interview should be used in combination with other assessment data to guide judgments about grades, determine placement in special programs, and make other important decisions about a student.

POWER OF ASSESSMENT INTERVIEWS

One of the benefits of using assessment interviews is that they provide important information that is useful for planning future instruction. As we illustrated here, this is true when thinking about individual students. After an assessment interview with one student, the teacher should be able to plan assignments or lessons that would support that student's learning. At other times, the teacher might use interview responses to develop understanding about why most of the class has done poorly on a test or some other assessment related to an area of learning. An interview with just a few students can often not only provide insight into the individual student difficulties but also identify misunderstandings or deficiencies that are affecting most students' performance. The teacher could plan new lessons for the entire class based on what she learns from interviewing just a few individuals.

Interviews are also useful when assessing very young children. For example, after having children draw a picture of a community helper, a kindergarten teacher might interview students by saying, "Tell me about your picture." Without the child's oral translation, the teacher may not know or understand the significance of the artwork in light of what a student knows about community helpers. The interview, therefore, becomes an essential part of the assessment of that child's learning.

Teachers of students who have special needs also find interviews to be an important assessment tool. Imagine a teacher who asks students to write a story so he can assess their ability to sequence events and organize ideas. The written work of a child who has a severe learning disability may evidence places where words, phrases, and even whole sentences are omitted. In an interview, the teacher may find that the student is actually able to compose a wonderfully sequenced and detailed story, but the written work would not reveal this ability.

Most chapters in this book discuss assessment approaches in which a student's work has to speak for itself. The fascinating part of the interview as an assessment tool is that the student has the opportunity to elaborate and expound on ideas. If a student does not understand a question, she can ask for clarification. At the same time, when student answers are not responsive to the question or are incomplete, the teacher has the opportunity—and perhaps the responsibility—to ask further questions to clarify whether the difficulty is a lack of knowledge or a misinterpretation of the question. The interview is an important strategy for assessing learning that cannot be assessed in other ways. The use of the interview can add important depth to a teacher's understanding of what a student knows and is able to do.

8 | A MULTIFACETED ASSESSMENT SYSTEM

Throughout this book, we have described a variety of assessments and explained their strengths and limitations. In this chapter, we offer suggestions about how to pull all these assessments together into a single, multifaceted assessment system. Such a synthesis is useful for a variety of purposes. Clearly, such rich information will allow teachers to more accurately determine what students have learned and to assign grades on report cards that reflect that learning. During conferences with students or their family members, having a variety of performance indicators can facilitate better communication and help the student and family understand what the student's accomplishments and challenges have been. A multifaceted assessment system also supports and guides teachers in planning instruction for their class and for individuals. In addition, teachers' referrals of students for special programs—either remedial or enrichment—will be less open to question if a full range of assessment information is the basis of the teacher's recommendation.

When only a single assessment strategy is used in the classroom, teachers may make judgments about student learning that are based as much on the interaction of the individual student with the form of the assessment as on what the student has actually learned. To ensure that teachers are measuring student learning and determining each student's strengths and weaknesses, it is important for teachers to use a variety of assessment strategies. This comprehensive approach to assessment will enable the teacher to paint a broader and more complete picture of the learning that has taken place and will better help the teacher identify those areas that may need to be reinforced to ensure student success. Figure 8–1 illustrates the variety of possibilities, as described in this book, from which teachers may choose when designing a multifaceted approach to assessment.

It is not practical to use all of these assessment formats. Teachers will want to start out using a few, beginning with those that are most comfortable and understandable. Gradually the teacher can add other formats to her assessment repertoire. The goal is to create a well-balanced assessment

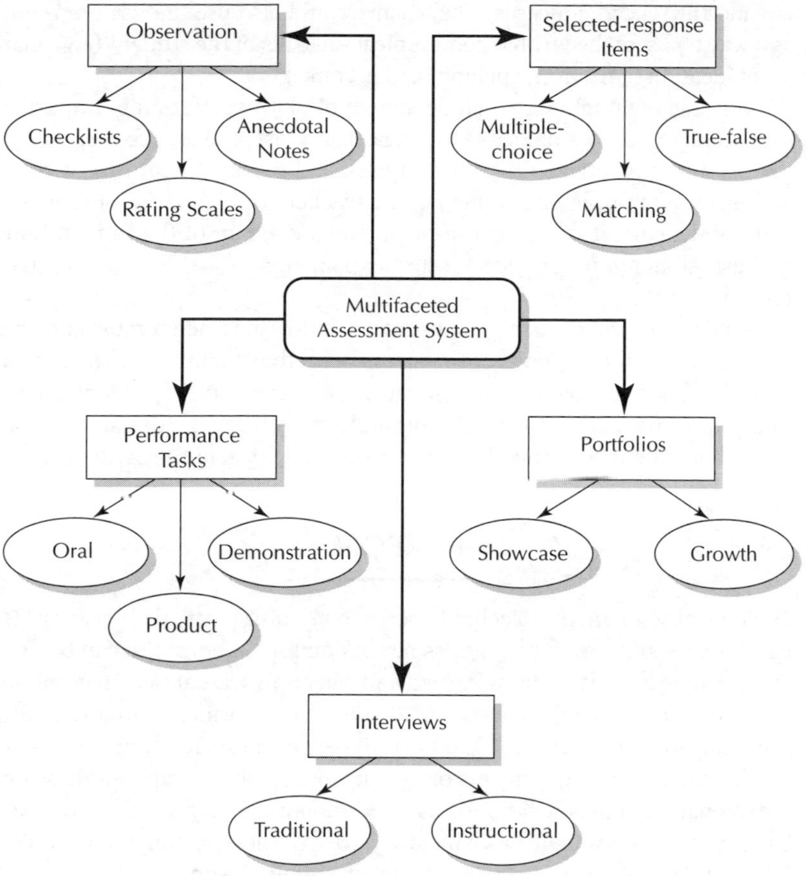

FIGURE 8–1   *Multifaceted assessment system*

system that enables all students to demonstrate what they know and what they can do.

In reality, most teachers will not be starting from scratch. Many of the activities that have always been done in the classroom can become the data for assessment of learning. Consider the seventh-grade science teacher who wants to assess learning about the systems of the body. During lab activities in which students examine the systems of different animals using models, the teacher could use observational checklists to record how individual students carry out the laboratory activity and complete the assignment.

She could also assign students the writing of a formal lab report in which they would describe the purpose, the procedures they used, and the observations they made and draw appropriate conclusions. In grading these reports, she would look for the completeness and accuracy of the information provided and clear conclusions that indicate the student understood the lab and the related concepts. The teacher could also use the written report as a way to assess the written communication skills of the student (e.g., clarity of ideas, organization, spelling, and grammar).

Assessment might also include more typical forms of testing. Important terminology (e.g., the names of the organs and systems) and concepts (e.g., the relationship between the cells, organs, and systems) could be assessed with several multiple-choice items. The teacher could also ask students to identify the correct placement of organs on a diagram of the human body and ask students to provide written explanations to a few constructed-response items.

In deciding which assessment strategy to use, the teacher must consider several factors: the purpose of the assessment, the alignment with curriculum, the time available for the assessment, and the issue of student opportunity to learn. Each of these factors influences teachers' decisions about what should be incorporated into the assessment system they will use.

PURPOSE

The type of assessment a teacher chooses to use on a particular occasion depends on the purpose for the assessment. A multiple-choice test can be used to determine if students have learned and can apply factual information, but it would not be useful in assessing a student's performance in a dramatic skit. Similarly, teachers can use observational checklists to observe students conducting science experiments or interacting in a play group, but these observational checklists will not measure a student's ability to write an essay. Each type of assessment has strengths and weaknesses, and each serves a different purpose when measuring what students know and can do. A teacher's decision to use a particular assessment form should be guided by an understanding of the purposes, strengths, and weaknesses of the approach.

ALIGNMENT OF CURRICULUM, INSTRUCTION, AND ASSESSMENT

There are lots of tests out there. How easy it would be for a teacher to teach her social studies lesson and then give a test from a teacher's manual or one that a colleague had used previously. This approach to finding a test, however, may not result in an assessment of the important ideas, concepts, and skills that the teacher emphasized in her classroom. The textbook company's view of what should be tested may not align with district curriculum guides, and even teachers in the same building may emphasize different topics that are appropriate for students in their classrooms but not a focus for students in other classes.

To really learn about students' knowledge and skills, the test should be aligned to the curriculum and assess the particular topics a teacher emphasized during instruction. This does not mean telling students the test items ahead of time, nor does it mean that a teacher must *specifically* teach what the test items ask. What we mean by alignment is that students have been taught the information and thinking skills they need to be successful on the classroom assessment that will be used. Such teaching of the content and skills needed to pass a test is appropriate if the teacher has reviewed the district's curriculum and designed instruction that matches the curriculum rather than disregarding the curriculum and only teaching test items.

TIME AND ASSESSMENT

Another consideration in deciding what type of assessment to use is the issue of how much classroom time can be used for the assessment. We have all taken tests in which a fixed time limit was provided. These "speeded" tests require students to work quickly, and, in many cases, students are not expected to complete all questions. If the purpose of the test is to compare students to one another, and that includes identifying those students who can answer correctly the most items in a short period of time, then speeded tests are appropriate.

Most of the time, however, classroom assessment is used to determine how well students have learned what has been taught. In these cases, students should be given sufficient time to complete the assessment. The use of performance tasks like those described in Chapter 3 must be weighed against the issue of classroom time. The benefits of performing the task must be balanced against the loss of time for instruction, as well as the out-of-class time students might need to invest to complete an assessment activity.

If the teacher is planning a test that must be completed within a forty-minute class period, there will not be sufficient time for students to plan, draft, and finalize a composition they are asked to write in response to a prompt. Similarly, the number of multiple-choice items a student can complete in this time period will depend upon the length of the questions. If the questions are simple factual recall items, a general rule of thumb is one minute per question. However, if the items require mathematics computation and include multistep problems, the test should include fewer items.

Preparing students for tests takes time as well. It is inappropriate for students to be expected to complete an assessment with no prior experience with the types of tasks they will encounter. Prior to a testing situation, students should know the kind of assessment they will be expected to complete, and such tasks should be part of their instructional experience. But teachers should not overdo it. Test item practice does not replace good instruction focused on the content and skills students are expected to learn.

Time also matters in terms of how much is available for the teacher to score the papers. If the assessment is the final exam of the year and the teacher must score the exams of eighty students and turn grades in the next morning, the teacher will not have time to carefully grade an assessment that includes six essays. A mixed assessment of selected-respone items (multiple-choice, true-false, matching) and a few constructed-response items can be scored in a relatively short period of time.

OPPORTUNITY TO LEARN

One of the responsibilities teachers have is to ensure their students are prepared for assessments outside the classroom and outside the control of the teacher, be they district, state, or national expectations for student performance. At times, these assessments may seem at odds with what the teacher believes is best for the students in his classroom. Balancing the various required tests with a multifaceted classroom assessment system is a challenge.

If the district or state requires students to participate in certain assessments, teachers must ensure that students are prepared for them. The classroom curriculum must include the standards or goals the required tests are based on. This does not mean limiting course content to that which will be assessed by the required test. Teachers have an obligation to provide students with the opportunity to learn the content and skills that will be tested. However, as time permits, the curriculum should be expanded to include content beyond what is on the test so that students can continue to learn and achieve beyond minimum expectations.

Teachers must also ensure that students are prepared for the types of test items they will encounter. As we discussed earlier, teachers should provide some practice to students so that they are prepared to handle test items. As the stakes are raised, teachers often feel pressured to increase test scores. To many teachers, raising test scores means practicing test items. Imagine spending days, weeks, even months doing little more than practicing test items in preparation for the "big test." Just as it is inappropriate for teachers to provide students with the answers to test items, it is also inappropriate to spend significant amounts of instructional time reviewing old test items from previous or sample tests in preparation for a required test.

Even in the high-stakes environment of a required test, teachers should continue to use a variety of assessment strategies in their classrooms so that they can more accurately assess student learning. When students are only assessed using a single type of assessment, they are cheated out of opportunities to learn how to perform on other forms of assessment. For example, students who spend most of their elementary and middle school education selecting an answer from a given list of four alternatives will be ill prepared to write the conclusion for a science laboratory experiment or to write a critical analysis of a character in a play.

As we stated earlier, practicing test items is not a substitute for quality instruction. Students will be successful on required assessments if they have been provided the following:

- a curriculum that incorporates the content and skills assessed by the required test
- high-quality, focused instruction aligned to that curriculum
- classroom assessments aligned to the curriculum and instruction
- an opportunity to have experience with the types of test items on the required test

STUDENT PROGRESS REPORTS

After all the assessments are administered and scored, the last task remaining is to report the student's progress. In the primary grades, one method for reporting student performance is through the use of some form of checklist. A teacher could use a checklist that has all the major concepts and skills expected for a second grader and check off those the child has learned. A short written summary statement at the bottom of the form would provide parents with a sense of how the student is doing overall.

Another approach is to use a similar form with sections for each reporting period. Within a reporting period, the teacher could indicate if the student has mastered the content or skill, is making progress toward mastery, or is just beginning to learn it. At the end of the year, the form would contain a record of each report that was sent home and show the student's progress across the entire school year.

In schools where more traditional grading approaches are used, the report of student progress takes a different form. If a teacher has administered five multiple-choice tests, each one with a maximum score of 100 points, the final grade is the average of these scores. Determining the grade when a variety of assessments are used is a bit more interesting.

One possible approach is to place scores from different assessments on a common scoring scheme and create a chart that shows the value of each grading scale. Figure 8–2 shows that a numerical grade between 90 and 100

Numerical Grade	Rubric Score	Letter Grade
90–100	4	A
80–89	3	B

FIGURE 8–2　*Chart comparing scoring methods*

is the same as a rubric score of 4 or a letter grade of A. At the end of the grading period a teacher would convert scores from all assessment tasks using this chart before finding the average.

In upper grade levels, a more complex approach might allow teachers to recognize that some assessments cover a broader and more significant range of content than others. The first task, in such a case, is to determine the relative weight of each assessment. Is an essay scored on a four-point rubric of equal weight to a multiple-choice test with fifty items? Does a showcase portfolio carry more weight than an end-of-term test? The teacher must make these decisions and, ideally, should tell students how everything counts. Once the teacher decides how much weight each assessment carries, then she must convert each score to the same scale.

Students in a sixth-grade language arts class might complete the assessments listed in Figure 8–3. If student grades were based on a mere sum of the scores they received, they might earn 300 points from multiple-choice tests and only 36 points on book reports. A teacher might feel that student performance on the book reports should be worth more than a single multiple-choice exam. By using a weighting factor, the score on book reports can be increased to make that student work have a greater effect on the final grade.

Assessments	Number	Possible Score	Weighting	Weighted Score	Total Score
Multiple-Choice Tests	3	100 points	1	100 points each	300 points
Book Reports	3	12 points	4	48 points each	144 points
Homework Assignments	10	10 points	1	10 points each	100 points
Class Presentation	1	5 points	20	100 points	100 points
Original Poem	2	15 points	4	60 points each	120 points
Autobiography	1	16 points	4	64 points each	64 points
Total					828 points

FIGURE 8–3   *Grade summary for language arts class*

In the example in Figure 8–3, the teacher decided to weight the book report with a factor of 4. Thus each book report is worth 48 points (12 points from the rubric score × 4 from the weighting factor = 48 as a weighted score). Since there were three book reports during the term, the total possible score for book reports would be 3 × 48, or 144. The result of this weighting is that the three book reports (144 points) now count almost half as much as the three tests (300 points). The teacher in the example used a weighting factor of 20 for the class presentation, making that task equivalent to a test (100 points). A weighting factor of 4 was used to weight the scores for the poem and the autobiography, thus increasing the effect of these tasks on the final grade.

To determine a student's grade, the teacher would divide the number of points the student earned by 828 and multiply by 100. For example, Maria earned 780 points. To determine her average, take $780 \div 828 \times 100 = 94.2$. In Maria's school, 94.2 is considered a grade of A.

Another teacher might convert all scores to letters and then average them according to a procedure provided by the school. The possibilities are endless. What matters is that the teacher's decision for the method to use is made after careful consideration of the types and importance of each assessment. The system also needs to be clear enough to explain to students and parents, and, most importantly, it must be applied fairly to all students.

Assessments should matter. If they don't, why give them? It serves no purpose for students and their teacher to spend time on a meaningless or useless assessment. How much the assessment matters is another issue. We live in a high-stakes environment where assessments are used to make critical decisions about students—graduation, promotion/retention, special programs, university acceptance. A single test score should not be used for making these high-stakes decisions. Because of the ramifications for students, teachers need to gather a variety of evidence to support their decisions about student performance. Use of the multifaceted approach recommended in this book provides a basis for accurate assessment of what students know and are able to do.

APPENDIX

Sites from school districts that give sample performance assessments

http://intranet.cps.k12.il.us/Assessments/Ideas_and_Rubrics/
    ideas_and_rubrics.html
http://www.open.k12.or.us/os98/4jperform
http://www.4j.lane.edu/instruction/cando/index.html

Sites associated with state and national projects

http://www.pals.sri.com
http://www.pattonville.k12.mo.us/services/assessment/showme.html

Other sites

http://school.discovery.com/schrockguide/index.html
http://www.ite.sc.edu/ite/ceasl.htm#tasksites

REFERENCES

Airasian, P. 1997. *Classroom Assessment*. 3d ed. New York: McGraw-Hill.

American Association for the Advancement of Science (AAAS). 1993. *Benchmarks for Science Literacy*. New York: Oxford.

American Heritage Dictionary. 1983. New York: Dell.

Bentley, M., C. Ebert, and E. Ebert. 2000. *The Natural Investigator: A Constructivist Approach to Teaching Elementary and Middle School Science*. Belmont, CA: Wadsworth/Thomson Learning.

Bloom, B., M. Englehart, E. Furst, W. Hill, and D. Krathwohl. 1956. *Taxonomy of Educational Objectives. Handbook 1. Cognitive Domains*. New York: McKay.

Brown, A., J. Campione, L. Webber, and K. McGilly. 1992. "Interactive Learning Environments: A New Look at Assessment and Instruction." In *Changing Assessments: Alternative Views of Aptitude, Achievement, and Instruction*, ed. B. Gifford and M. O'Connor. Boston: Kluwer Academic.

Byers, B. 1970. *The Summer of the Swans*. New York: Viking Kestrel.

Chase, C. 1968. "The Impact of Some Obvious Variables on Essay Test Scores." *Journal of Educational Measurement* 5: 315–18.

———. 1979. "The Impact of Achievement Expectations and Handwriting Quality on Scoring Essay Tests." *Journal of Educational Measurement* 16: 39–42.

———. 1986. "Essay Test Scoring: Interaction of Relevant Variables." *Journal of Educational Measurement* 23: 33–41.

Ebert, C., and E. Ebert II. 1998. *The Inventive Mind on Science: Creative Thinking Activities*. Englewood, CA: Teacher Ideas.

Feuerstein, R., Y. Rand, M. Jensen, S. Kaniel, and D. Tzuriel. 1987. "Prerequisites for Assessment of Learning Potential: The LPAD Model." In *Dynamic Assessment: An Interactional Approach to Evaluating Learning Potential*, ed. C. Lidz, 35–51. New York: Guilford.

Gipson, F. 1956. *Old Yeller*. New York: Harper Trophy.

Goodwin, W., and L. Driscoll. 1980. *Handbook for Measurement and Evaluation in Early Childhood Education*. San Francisco: Jossey-Bass.

Gredler, M. 1999. *Classroom Assessment and Learning.* New York: MacMillan.

Haladyna, T. 1997. *Writing Test Items to Evaluate Higher Order Thinking.* Needham Heights, MA: Allyn & Bacon.

Hales, L., and E. Tokar. 1975. "The Effect of the Quality of Preceding Responses on the Grades Assigned to Subsequent Responses to an Essay Question." *Journal of Educational Measurement* 12: 115–18.

Harrington, H., S. Meisels, P. McMahon, M. Dichtelmiller, and J. Jablon. 1997. *Observing, Documenting, and Assessing Learning: The Work Sampling System Handbook for Teacher Educators.* Ann Arbor, MI: Rebus.

Herman, J., P. Aschbacher, and L. Winters. 1992. *A Practical Guide to Alternative Assessment.* Alexandria, VA: Association for Supervision and Curriculum Development.

Hughes, D., B. Keeling, and B. Tuck. 1980. "The Influence of Context Position and Scoring Method on Essay Scoring." *Journal of Educational Measurement* 17: 131–36.

Jablon, J., L. Ashley, D. Marsden, S. Meisels, and M. Dichtelmiller. 1994. *Omnibus Guidelines: Kindergarten Through Fifth Grade.* 3d ed. Ann Arbor, MI: Rebus.

Kuhs, T. 1992. *Mathematics Assessment: Alternative Approaches.* Reston, VA: National Council of Teachers of Mathematics.

———. 1997. *Measure for Measure: Using Portfolios in K–8 Mathematics.* Portsmouth, NH: Heinemann.

L'Engle, M. 1998. *A Wrinkle in Time.* Thorndike, ME: G. K. Hall.

Meisels, S., F. Liaw, A. Dorfman, and R. Nelson. 1995. "The Work Sampling System: Reliability and Validity of a Performance Assessment for Young Children." *Early Childhood Research Quarterly* 10: 277–96.

Messick, S. 1995. "Validity of Psychological Assessment: Validation of Inferences from Person's Responses and Performances as Scientific Inquiry into Score Meaning." *American Psychologist* 50 (9): 741–49.

Mills, H. 1990. "Teachers and Children: Partners in Learning." In *Portraits of Whole Language Classrooms,* ed. H. Mills and J. Clyde, 43–63. Portsmouth, NH: Heinemann.

National Council of Teachers of English (NCTE) and International Reading Association (IRA). 1996. *Standards of the English Language Arts.* Urbana, IL: NCTE and IRA.

National Council of Teachers of Mathematics (NCTM). 2000. *Principles and Standards for School Mathematics.* Reston, VA: NCTM.

National Research Council. 1999. *High Stakes: Testing for Tracking, Promotion, and Graduation.* Washington, DC: National Academy Press.

New Standards Project. 1992. *Aquarium Task.* Rochester, New York: National Center on Education and the Economy.

New York State Education Department (NYSED). 1988. *Regents Competency Test in Science.* Albany, NY: NYSED.

————. 1989. *Improving the Classroom Test.* Albany, NY: State University of New York Press.

Nicolson, S., and S. G. Shipstead. 1994. *Through the Looking Glass: Observations in the Early Childhood Classroom.* New York: MacMillan.

Nitko, A. 1996. *Educational Assessment of Students.* 2d ed. Englewood Cliffs, NJ: Merrill-Prentice Hall.

Olson, J., L. Bond, and C. Andrews. 1999. *Annual Survey of State Student Assessment Programs: A Summary Report.* Washington, DC: Council of Chief State School Officers.

Osterlind, S. J. 1998. *Constructing Test Items: Multiple-Choice, Constructed-Response, Performance, and Other Formats.* Boston: Kluwer Academic.

Paterson, K. 1977. *Bridge to Terabithia.* New York: HarperCollins.

Paulsen, G. 1987. *Hatchet.* New York: Simon & Schuster.

Popham, W. 1978. *Criterion Referenced Measurement.* Englewood Cliffs, NJ: Prentice-Hall.

Resnick, L., and D. Resnick. 1992. "Assessing the Thinking Curriculum: New Tools for Educational Reform." In *Changing Assessments: Alternative Views of Aptitude, Achievement, and Instruction,* ed. B. Gifford and M. O'Connor, 37–75. Boston: Kluwer Academic.

Rhodes, L., and N. Shanklin. 1993. *Windows into Literacy: Assessing Learners K–8.* Portsmouth, NH: Heinemann.

Shavelson, R., G. Baxter, and X. Gao. 1993. "Sampling Variability of Performance Assessments." *Journal of Educational Measurement* 30 (3): 215–32.

South Carolina State Department of Education (SCSDE). 1998a. *Reading/English Language Arts: South Carolina Grade-by-Grade Standards.* Columbia, SC: SCSDE.

————. 1998b. *South Carolina Curriculum Standards for Science.* Columbia, SC: SCSDE.

————. 1999. *PACT Reading/English Language Arts Assessment: A Blueprint for Success.* Columbia, SC: SCSDE.

Spandel, V., and R. Culham. 1994. *Creating a Portfolio: A Workshop Handout.* Portland, OR: Northwest Regional Education Laboratory.

Taylor, C. 1997. *A Wrinkle in Time.* <http://www.desconnect.com/ctaylor/Cides/egowman/Wrinkle/intro.htm>.

Taylor, M. 1976. *Roll of Thunder, Hear My Cry.* New York: Bantam Books.

Vygotsky, L. 1978. *Mind in Society: The Development of Higher Psychological Processes,* ed. M. Cole, V. John-Steiner, S. Scribner, and E. Souberman. Cambridge, MA: Harvard University Press.

Wiggins, G. 1993. "Assessment: Authenticity, Context, and Validity." *Phi Delta Kappan* (November): 200–14.

Worthen, B., K. White, F. Xitao, and R. Sudweeks. 1999. *Measurement and Assessment in Schools.* New York: Addison Wesley Longman.